# SAVEUR

# THE WAY WE COOK

# SAVEUR

# THE WAY WE COOK

## Portraits from Around the World

**EDITED BY JAMES OSELAND**

**INTRODUCTION BY FRANCINE PROSE**

**LOS ANGELES, CALIFORNIA** Home cook Marino Pascal with a plate of hortopita, fennel and herb phyllo pastries. *Photograph by James Oseland*

To cook is to lay hands on the body of the world.

—John Thorne, in *Simple Cooking*

MEXICO CITY, MEXICO In the sprawling Merced market, a team of food vendors prepares a variety of snacks. *Photograph by Penny De Los Santos*

# FOREWORD

COOKING CONNECTS US. As you look at the photographs of cooks around the world assembled in this book, maybe that notion will appear obvious. I hope so. From the first issue of SAVEUR, back in 1994, we have traced the vital links that food provides—among families, within cultures, even between strangers—in the stories, the recipes, and most definitely, the photographs we publish. What we make is a magazine about cooking, but what readers have come to expect from SAVEUR is photography so vivid and real that it brings the world, in all its hectic, human, sauce-splattered magnificence, into sharper focus.

Still, for those of us who edit SAVEUR, creating this book was revelatory. We began by looking at articles from the past decade, and it was moving to trace their common threads. Even when two stories were about cooks on opposite sides of the planet, one working over an open fire, the other at a restaurant stove, they depicted a shared humanity. The photographs gathered here are the ones that stopped us in our tracks. Some ran in the magazine; others were outtakes that deserve to be seen. In them we see people putting food on the table—in homes and restaurants, in markets and on city streets, in landscapes seemingly untouched by the passage of time. At the end of the book, we've included a selection of recipes from the original stories. Sharing food is central to what we do at SAVEUR, just as it is central to the lives we glimpse in the pages that follow.

We are able to grasp that thanks to the skill and sensitivity of the photographers, some of SAVEUR's most trusted contributors, who frame these scenes so that we see the food, and see beyond it. Look closely, and see a microcosm take shape around the person at the stove. In feeding us, in keeping alive the flavors that define a cuisine and a culture, cooks tell us not only who they are, but who we are. With this book, we offer our heartfelt admiration. —*James Oseland,* SAVEUR *Editor-in-Chief*

9

**MUANG SING, LAOS** In the early morning, a hawker prepares *khao soi*, rice noodle soup garnished with pork and blanched greens. *Photograph by Naomi Duguid*

# INTRODUCTION

HOW OLD WAS I WHEN some helpful adult made it clear that cooking wasn't actually magic? I can't quite remember. Before that I'd somehow imagined that my mom, in her apron, preparing the greatest hits of 1950s American cuisine, sprinkling the canned, deep-fried onions over the French-cut green beans with creamy mushroom soup, might as well have been performing with a top hat, a cape, and a magic wand. It wasn't as if I didn't spend plenty of time in our Brooklyn kitchen, watching my mother and the stellar Southern cooks—first Cleo, then Delia, then Kathy—my parents hired to take care of us when they were away at work. But the miracle of transformation that turned a raw chicken into something sublimely delicious, crispy, salty, and Southern-fried seemed closer to sleight of hand than any visible step-by-step process involving buttermilk, flour, and oil.

By now I understand that cooking involves skills that can be learned, practiced, repeated; that it is a science as well an art. And as I've grown older and traveled the world, enjoying street food, dining in restaurants, cooking and eating with family and friends, I've come to recognize that for the cook and the lucky recipient of the cook's generosity, energy, and expertise, the pleasures of cooking—sensory, physical, spiritual, aesthetic, and communal, to name just a few—not only last longer but sustain and thrill us more than the rabbit popping out of the hat.

All the steamy, hands-on magic of cooking rises from the stew pots, grills, griddles, frying pans, fires, and kettles that bubble and smoke away in the colorful pages of this book, a loving celebration of cooking all over the world, of people cooking alone and in groups, domestically and professionally, on the street, in their homes, in restaurants, bus stops, and back yards. It is a tribute to the ways in which our fellow humans make food we want to eat—an apparently simple idea that, when you think about it for a moment, resonates on so many levels. Sorting through its pages, you can feel the strength of the woman hefting a pork shoulder at Helen's Bar-B-Q in Brownsville, Tennessee, and admire the way she imbues her plastic hairnet with the dignity of a chef's toque. You can bask in the jaw-dropping confidence of the young Turkish chef rolling out phyllo dough as a crowd looks on, the playful confrontation in the penetrating stare of the grill guy in Jerusalem, the luminous faces of three Iranian women who have brought their cooking pots out into the street.

Thinking a bit harder, you may find yourself wondering why there aren't more books like this, books in which the focus broadens from the handsome food on the table to the people who make it. My husband, the main cook in the family, is a passionate cookbook collector. I like to look through his cookbooks, which to me are more like fashion magazines, images of future fantasies that may or may not come true. Every so often it crosses my mind that if I were a Martian or an archeologist from the future, I would have trouble figuring out, judging only from the evidence of cookbooks, how that bowl of glossy pasta got there in front of the Cathedral of Orvieto. Who made the paella in the pan so large it takes up a two-page spread, posed against the lovely Spanish tiles of an empty kitchen?

SAVEUR's *The Way We Cook* reminds us of the fact that food is cooked by people. This is what they look like, this is how they work, these are the places they cook in, all over the world, and the friends and relations with whom they prepare and enjoy a meal. You want to look at each of these pictures for a long time, thinking about the subjects and the little narrative that each photo is telling. It's a rare pleasure to consider the delicate contemplation of the woman whose gaze lingers over two plates of stir-fried food in Singapore, the placid loveliness of an Ethiopian cook lifting the lid off a griddle on which she is preparing bread. A pleasure, too, is the chance to witness the sheer ebullience of a Brazilian man compelled to raise both arms in a joyous, impromptu celebration at the promise of a small feast. Or to admire the grace of the Venetian woman who appears to be dancing with the sun flooding through her kitchen window.

But what you really want is to be inside these pictures. You want to eat the food: the fried pork chop and the mac and cheese; the stir-fry, the scrambled eggs, the pineapple upside-down cake. And to revel in how beautiful the subjects look, caught in the private, semi-private, and public act of preparing or serving something appealing. The longer we look at these photos, the more likely we are to find ourselves thinking that there's something magnetic in itself about competence and know-how in the kitchen. How can we not marvel at the assurance with which the Bolognese pasta-maker threads her fingers through a cat's cradle of golden noodles? Or at the precision and focus of the pedigreed Viennese pastry chefs creating elaborate chocolate-dipped pastries from what we must assume are the finest ingredients, chosen with the greatest of care? We may have been taught that pride is a deadly sin, but these cooks make pride seem like a totally justified and sympathetic emotion.

*The Way We Cook* zooms in on something that's been overlooked, or underlooked, despite the fact that the act of cooking is something all of us see at some point, every day! It whisks us from kitchen to kitchen without making us leave home. It can't give us all the pleasures of flavor, for instance, and smell. For that, we'll want to make these dishes ourselves, or give the book to friends who cook, or travel to places far away to find these foods. The photos collected here confirm what I thought as a child: that cooking really is magic. It's a widely available magic, as we gather from these pages that prove how endlessly different we are, and, when we are cooking, how deliciously alike.

—*Francine Prose,* SAVEUR *Contributing Editor*

**CHARLESTON, SOUTH CAROLINA**
Chef Debra Gadsden serves up a fried pork chop, macaroni and cheese, and okra soup at her family's restaurant, Martha Lou's Kitchen. *Photograph by Todd Coleman*

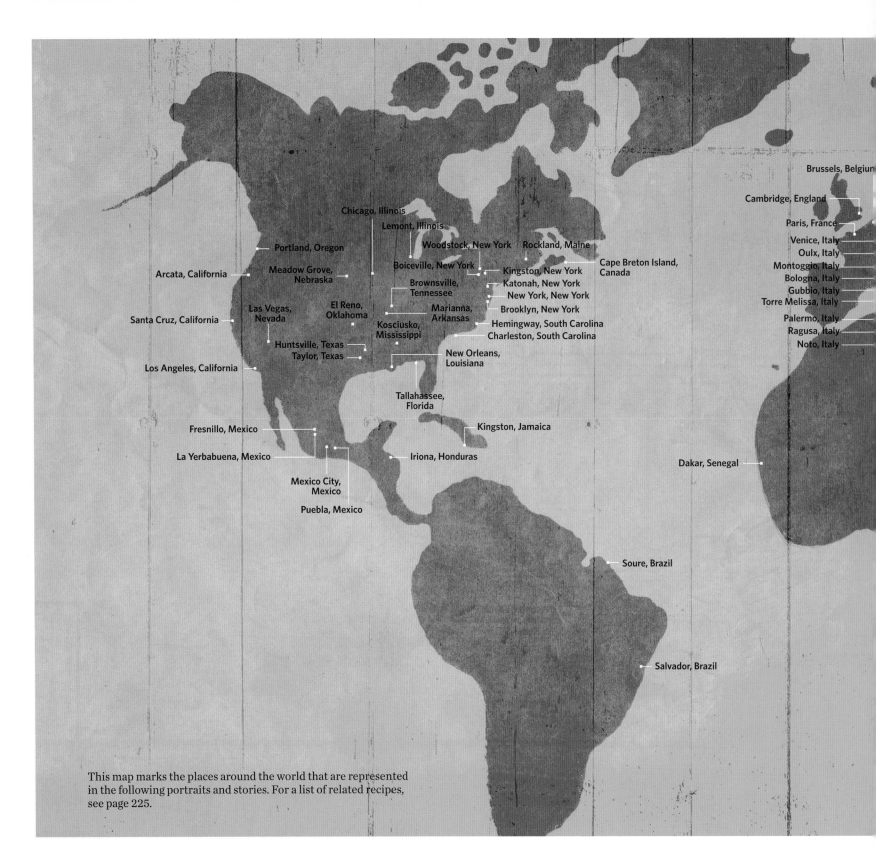

Brussels, Belgium

Cambridge, England

Paris, France

Venice, Italy
Oulx, Italy
Montoggio, Italy
Bologna, Italy
Gubbio, Italy
Torre Melissa, Italy
Palermo, Italy
Ragusa, Italy
Noto, Italy

Chicago, Illinois
Lemont, Illinois
Woodstock, New York
Rockland, Maine
Portland, Oregon
Boiceville, New York
Cape Breton Island, Canada
Kingston, New York
Arcata, California
Meadow Grove, Nebraska
Brownsville, Tennessee
Katonah, New York
New York, New York
Las Vegas, Nevada
El Reno, Oklahoma
Marianna, Arkansas
Brooklyn, New York
Santa Cruz, California
Kosciusko, Mississippi
Hemingway, South Carolina
Charleston, South Carolina
Huntsville, Texas
Taylor, Texas
New Orleans, Louisiana
Los Angeles, California
Tallahassee, Florida
Fresnillo, Mexico
Kingston, Jamaica
La Yerbabuena, Mexico
Iriona, Honduras
Dakar, Senegal
Mexico City, Mexico
Puebla, Mexico
Soure, Brazil
Salvador, Brazil

This map marks the places around the world that are represented
in the following portraits and stories. For a list of related recipes,
see page 225.

Stockholm, Sweden

Launkalne, Latvia

Riga, Latvia

Vissani, Greece

Vienna, Austria

Viscri, Romania

Miklósvár, Romania

Bucharest, Romania

Istanbul, Turkey

Pigádi, Greece

Gaziantep, Turkey

Qazvin, Iran

Hatay, Turkey

Tehran, Iran

Beirut, Lebanon

Isfahan, Iran

Jerusalem, Israel

Beijing, China

Kyoto, Japan

Paphos, Cyprus

Chengdu, China

Suzhou, China

Crotone, Italy

Delhi, India

Muang Sing, Laos

Ahmedabad, India

Vientiane, Laos

Da Nang, Vietnam

Mumbai, India

Phung Hiep, Vietnam

Addis Ababa, Ethiopia

Thale Noi, Thailand

Singapore

Olangaianet, Kenya

Lamu, Kenya

Jakarta, Indonesia

**LAS VEGAS, NEVADA** At Bartolotta Ristorante di Mare, chef Paul Bartolotta ices down the fish of the day while sous chef Carlos Rodriguez looks on. *Photograph by Todd Coleman*

**MEADOW GROVE, NEBRASKA**
Carol and Rich Grant pause to pray
before breakfast on their hog farm.
*Photograph by Beth Rooney*

**SALVADOR, BRAZIL** Mareneusa de Jesus Salles (left) and Jubiraci Martins da Silva, with some of the ingredients for their lunch of grilled fish. *Photograph by Penny De Los Santos*

23

**RAGUSA, ITALY** Giovanna Giglio Cascone, a Sicilian home cook, prepares Easter dinner for her family. *Photograph by Landon Nordeman*

MASTERS OF

# THE FLAMES

27

I GREW UP IN CENTRAL GEORGIA, near Macon, one-half mile from Old Clinton Barbecue, a tin-roofed, sawdust-floored roadhouse shrouded in hickory smoke. Mittie Coulter, mother of proprietor Wayne Coulter, worked the chopping block. By the time my Schwinn hit the gravel parking lot, I could hear the measured and percussive thwack of her cleaver. It carried through the dining room, past Wayne's collection of antique cash registers, as she hacked fat and skin from hams, chopped the flesh to smoky bits, and doused it all with a thin, ketchup-tinged sauce that tasted of cider vinegar and red pepper. I can see the granny glasses Mrs. Coulter wore. I can see that cleaver, too, spangling beneath the overhead fluorescent lamp. But I can't picture the black men who worked for her, tending the massive pit out back, shoveling hardwood coals beneath those hams. From the time I was two until I left for college, at 17, I ate the food those pitmasters cooked: tender wood-smoked pork shoulder hacked and laid on white bread. I don't know their names. But they were culinary heroes, and barbecue—accomplished through arduous labor done by working-class folks, black and white—is not just a great national food. It's an art form. —*John T. Edge,* SAVEUR, June/July 2011

THE AMERICAN SOUTH Jimmy Brown, a cook at Scott's Bar-B-Que in Hemingway, South Carolina. *Photograph by Landon Nordeman*

THE AMERICAN SOUTH Sam
Thompson, a cook at Scott's Bar-B-
Que in Hemingway, South Carolina.
Facing page: Spencer Croker, a cook
at Scott's Bar-B-Que, with a whole
hog he is about to prepare for the pit.
*Photographs by Landon Nordeman*

**STOCKHOLM, SWEDEN** A cook at the café Vete-Katten prepares dozens of plates of the signature dish, *räksallad,* a shrimp salad. *Photograph by Todd Coleman*

**VISSANI, GREECE** Neighbors Maria Tsomokou and Zaharoula Basios carry dishes to a nearby hilltop for a picnic amid the wildflowers. *Photograph by James Oseland*

VENICE, ITALY Before sitting down to a meal, chef and cooking teacher Mara Martin welcomes the day in her kitchen in the Pisani Moretta, a palazzo on the Grand Canal. *Photograph by Penny De Los Santos*

**THALE NOI, THAILAND** At his food stall in this southern fishing village, Pornsawan Pattcha makes any number of classic Thai dishes. *Photograph by James Oseland*

**NEW YORK, NEW YORK** Chefs from a Brooklyn-based Hare Krishna temple dining hall prepare a vegetarian lunch in the SAVEUR kitchen with some of its staff members. *Photograph by James Oseland*

**PARIS, FRANCE** Students at Le Ferrandi culinary school take a break from practicing their sauce preparations. *Photograph by David Brabyn/ SIPA Press*

**KINGSTON, NEW YORK** Views of writer Bruce Littlefield's 1966 Airstream Overlander. Littlefield cooks his meals in the trailer's small kitchen as he travels the country with his dog, Westminster (far right). *Photographs by Landon Nordeman*

**IRIONA, HONDURAS** Garifuna cooks prepare cassava bread on the wood-burning clay stove of their village's communal kitchen. *Photograph by Penny De Los Santos*

LAS VEGAS, NEVADA A family
dinner at the home of Eatty Du,
who has prepared a spread of
dishes from her native Shanghai.
*Photograph by Todd Coleman*

BRUSSELS, BELGIUM A waiter flambés dessert crêpes at the Aux Armes de Bruxelles restaurant. *Photograph by Beth Rooney*

**DA NANG, VIETNAM** A cook at a countryside Buddhist temple stir-fries tofu for a lunch that will be served to the monastic community. *Photograph by Penny De Los Santos*

**ARCATA, CALIFORNIA** Chief John McFarland turns out a favorite but sticky dessert, pineapple upside-down cake, for his team of firefighters. *Photograph by Barbara Ries*

**BUCHAREST, ROMANIA** A woman fans the flames before grilling her family's lunch outside her apartment building in the city's center. *Photograph by Landon Nordeman*

**CHICAGO, ILLINOIS** A cook makes queso fresco and simmers tomatillos for salsa. A tortilla maker kneads 50 pounds of corn masa, and a manager accepts a delivery of a suckling pig, destined for a dish of achiote-marinated pork. All of these images show a typical morning in the shared kitchen of Frontera Grill and Topolobampo, the adjacent restaurants of chef Rick Bayless (pictured, top row, second from left, among other places), whose commitment to authenticity has helped educate American diners about Mexico's many regional cuisines. *Photographs by Penny De Los Santos*

63

**KINGSTON, NEW YORK** Joshua and Jessica Applestone at their shop, Fleisher's, where they butcher traditional cuts of meats and prepare sausages. *Photograph by Landon Nordeman*

CHENGDU, CHINA In the capital of Sichuan province, a street vendor grills an array of meats, seafood, and vegetables. *Photograph by Ariana Lindquist*

**TORRE MELISSA, ITALY** Sheep farmers and cheese makers Giovanni and Antonietta Bevilacqua. *Photograph by Landon Nordeman*

# THE SWEET LIFE

**VIENNA, AUSTRIA** Pastry chefs decorate Easter sweets at Demel, a 226-year-old pastry shop.
*Photograph by Landon Nordeman*

I INHALE DEEPLY AND AM MET with the scent of butter and sugar baking together. Before me a scene of intense but methodical activity takes place amid ovens and storage racks, a sheeter for rolling dough, mixers of several sizes, and yards and yards of wood and marble tabletops. In the kitchens of Vienna's 226-year-old Demel bakery, where almost every item—dense chocolate *sachertortes*, jam-filled *linzertortes*, strudels wrapped in papery-thin pastry, pastel-frosted petits fours—is shaped, filled, or decorated by hand, at these tables, or benches, as they are called, are bakers at work. One slices towering stacks of round cakes into layers. Another frosts a cake by holding it from below with her fingertips and maneuvering it to make it meet a spatula that she holds in her other hand. Workers pipe pastel flowers onto glossy cakes, while nearby a young apprentice rolls brioche dough into long cylinders and then shapes them into knots, braids, and other designs. A baker puts a thick slice of Demel's famous *trüffeltorte* onto a plate and hands it to me. The ganache filling is airy and light, in perfect contrast to the rich chocolate cake and bittersweet dusting of cocoa on top. As I savor the confection, I experience a heady mix of joy, inspiration, humility, and, most of all, gratitude—to Demel's bakers for bringing such sweet things to life. —*Nick Malgieri,* SAVEUR, *March 2009*

**VIENNA, AUSTRIA** Two customers admire the desserts on display at Demel, a celebrated bakery. *Photograph by Landon Nordeman*

**LEMONT, ILLINOIS** Thanksgiving Day in the kitchen of the Orozco family. *Photograph by Beth Rooney*

**WOODSTOCK, NEW YORK** Philippe Petit, who in 1974 walked a tightrope stretched between the towers of Manhattan's World Trade Center, enjoys a moment of whimsy in his home kitchen. *Photograph by Landon Nordeman*

**LOS ANGELES, CALIFORNIA** At The Bazaar by José Andres, a restaurant that serves both traditional and contemporary Spanish dishes, a sous-chef plates yogurt dip, fava beans, and cucumber. *Photograph by Ariana Lindquist*

**GAZIANTEP, TURKEY** Home cooks Selma Direkçi (left) and her daughter Sedra Özgüler share a laugh before a family lunch. *Photograph by Todd Coleman*

81

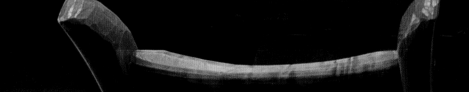
**KYOTO, JAPAN** A team of cooks prepares for service at Shojiki Naka-higashi, a restaurant specializing in local and foraged foods. *Photograph by Jun Takagi*

**EL RENO, OKLAHOMA** At left, Marty Hall, the owner of Sid's Diner, readies an order for a drive-though customer. At right, Sid's specialty, onion-fried burgers, on the grill. *Photographs by Penny De Los Santos*

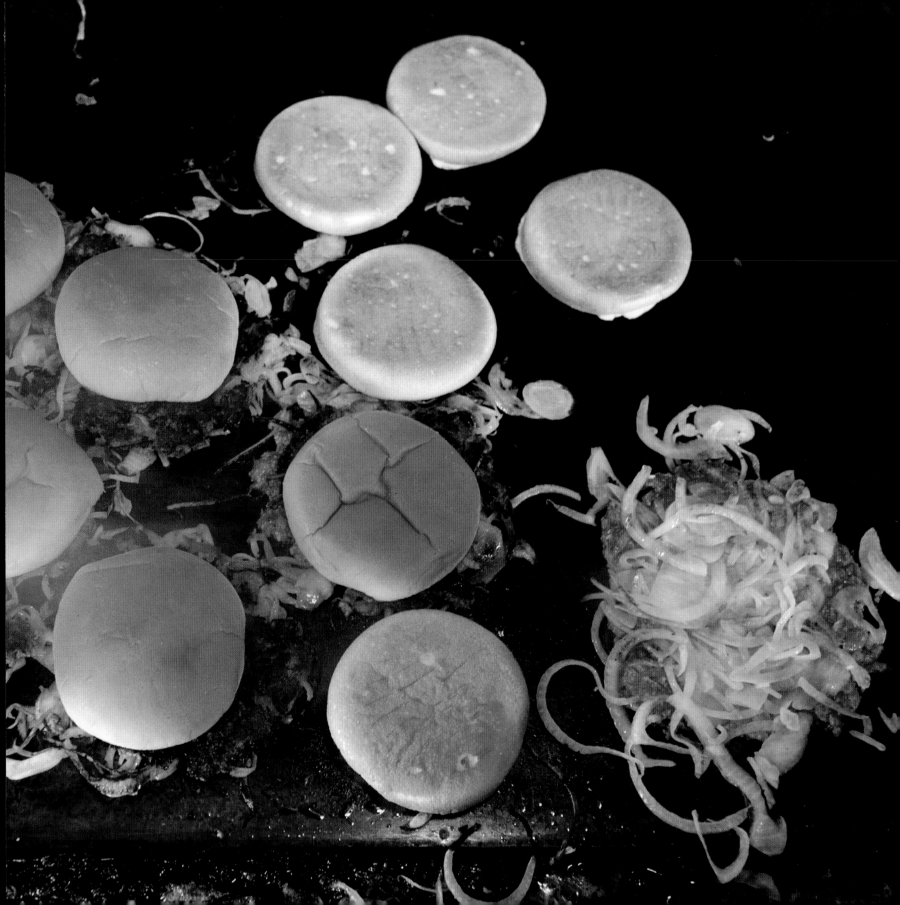

LAUNKALNE, LATVIA Maija Kalnins (foreground) with carrots from her garden heading home for lunch with her husband, Rich Kalnins, and their sons, Laris and Niklavs. *Photograph by Landon Nordeman*

**BROOKLYN, NEW YORK** During the holiday of Sukkot, when Orthodox Jewish men are prohibited from eating indoors, home cook Mendel Zirkind smells, but does not taste, the sauce he is making. *Photograph by Ariana Lindquist*

**PARIS, FRANCE** Scenes from a few time-honored Paris bistros, from left: a chef at the kitchen window of Le Bistrot Paul Bert; staff at Allard with a dish of roast duck with olives; steak tartare, a specialty of the house at Le Bistrot Paul Bert; chefs at work in the kitchen of Aux Lyonnais. *Photographs by Landon Nordeman*

**PIGADI, GREECE** Sisters-in-law Diamando Xerakia (left) and Stamatoula Moulyatis toast with homemade wine before a lunch of eggs scrambled with their own goats' milk cheese. *Photograph by Penny De Los Santos*

**ISTANBUL, TURKEY** A server at the beverage parlor Vefa Bozacisi fills glasses of *boza*, a fermented bulgur drink. *Photograph by Landon Nordeman*

# WHERE A GUEST EATS LIKE A KING

DAKAR · SENEGAL Khady Mbow (left) and her niece Sini prepare lunch for family and friends. *Photograph by Penny De Los Santos*

THE HEAT IS GATHERING, driving everyone indoors. It's midafternoon in Dakar, Senegal, and the foot traffic in this narrow, two-story home in the working-class Gibraltar neighborhood is seriously congested. More people arrive every minute—relatives, neighbors, an imam—and collapse in the dark, cool refuge of the living room. In a small kitchen off the courtyard, a handsome, tall woman named Khady Mbow puts the final touches on the *soupoukandia*, a fiery, gumbolike stew of okra, palm oil, Scotch bonnet peppers, and shellfish served over rice. She and her 30-year-old niece, Sini, have spent the morning pounding vegetables in a mortar and pestle, scraping the mash into a steaming pot and stirring relentlessly. The Gueyes own a food processor, but Khady—the family's matriarch and chief culinary architect—believes the mortar and pestle better preserve flavor. Everything is done by hand. Finally, Khady and Sini ladle the *soupoukandia* into a pair of large metal bowls and trundle them inside. Twenty or so people, including four generations of Gueyes, gather around the bowls, spoons hovering. Then Khady gives the order to eat in French, the country's official language: "Mangez!" The spicy

»

**DAKAR, SENEGAL** At a home in the southwestern part of the city, guests eat in the traditional way, from a communal bowl. *Photograph by Penny De Los Santos*

»

*soupoukandia* delivers a swift roundhouse kick, making noses run and sweat bead up on foreheads, but spoons continue to shovel away, clinking off the bottom of the bowls. The dish—sweet and sharp and hot all at once—elicits a chorus of contented grunts and lip-smacking. These are the best kinds of meals in Senegal: eaten at friends' houses, prepared in sparse courtyards by women and girls using little by way of equipment besides a mortar and pestle, some dull knives, a propane tank, and a small charcoal grill. Meals tend to be single-dish affairs, with everyone grazing from one bowl or platter, using spoons or bare hands to scoop up meat and vegetables, always supplemented with rice or couscous. Still, a guest in Senegal is treated like a king, given the best seat, the biggest cut of meat, and encouraged to eat until he or she is bursting. After a big meal—of *soupoukandia;* or *màfe,* a peanut stew made with chicken, fish, or lamb; or the national dish of *thiéboudienne,* rice, fish, and vegetables in a pungent, chile-hot tomato stew—guests linger while chatting in a cool, shady place as the early-evening sky turns a livid orange, and the muezzins sing out the call to prayer. —*John O'Connor,* SAVEUR, *May 2012*

**DAKAR, SENEGAL** Khady Mbow relaxes after serving lunch in her home. *Photograph by Penny De Los Santos*

**VIENTIANE, LAOS** At a Buddhist ceremony honoring departed ancestors, women prepare *laap moo,* a minced pork salad, for more than a hundred guests. *Photograph by Ariana Lindquist*

**ISTANBUL, TURKEY** A contestant at an annual competition for chefs who specialize in baklava rolls out phyllo dough as the press looks on. *Photograph by Todd Coleman*

Saare market

Law firm backs
RCOM bid for MTN

BHP Billiton, Usha Martin sign
agreement to tap Jharkhand mines

TVS

# EACH
# DISH IS
# AN ART

AHMEDABAD, INDIA A home cook drizzles clarified butter over freshly made chapati flatbreads. *Photograph by James Oseland*

V ARSHABEN CHAUHAN, THE WIFE of a taxi driver, lives in the old city of Ahmedabad, in the Indian state of Gujarat. She cooks squatting on her kitchen floor, cutting small red onions with a knife fashioned from a recycled band saw. There is no chopping board; whatever she has to cut—potatoes, tomatoes, chiles—she holds in her hand, letting slices fall onto a battered stainless-steel plate. She deftly dispenses with two fist-size cabbages, shredding them onto the plate and then massaging the cabbage with salt to soften it. Next she heats peanut oil and adds black mustard seeds, curry leaves, and the pungent spice asafetida. Almost every Gujarati dish begins like this: with the quick-frying of spices and aromatics, which release their essence into the cooking fat so that the flavors can infuse the ingredients that are added later. "You have to listen to the mustard seeds," Chauhan explains. "They'll tell you when to add the next ingredient." Sure enough, the seeds begin popping furiously, and when the noise subsides, she adds the cabbage along with slices of tomato and peppers. The finished dish, flavored with sweet jaggery, lime juice, and chopped cilantro, looks something like an Indian coleslaw. The cabbage is remarkably supple, and the dish

»

**AHMEDABAD, INDIA** Varshaben Chauhan in the kitchen of her apartment.
*Photograph by James Oseland*

110

»

delivers a full range of tastes—sweet, sour, bitter, salty, spicy—in every bite. It is proof that even the simplest of dishes can be made to sing in a carefully pitched harmony in Gujarat. Jutting into the Arabian Sea, this part of India was for centuries a center of trade with points west; it has also been a place where the traditions of North India and South India converge. A constant flow of new ingredients has moved through its port cities, and outside urban areas, much of Gujarat is farmland, so local produce is plentiful, too. The state is home to Hindus, Muslims, and members of numerous other religions and sects, notably the Jains, who follow a nonviolent way of life of which strict vegetarianism is a part. In fact, two out of every three Gujaratis do not eat meat. Beyond that restriction, though, Gujaratis are happy to indulge their appetites to glorious excess. How do Gujarati cooks manage to obtain such a range and depth of flavor from the vegetables they cook? That comes down in no small part to technique. The careful preparation, the considered seasoning, the variety of ingredients—every aspect of the dish adds up to a balanced and beautiful whole. —*Todd Coleman,* SAVEUR, *December 2009*

**AHMEDABAD, INDIA** Sangam Mehta (right), in the kitchen with her mother, Charu, breaking up lentil flatbread to add to a curry. *Photograph by James Oseland*

**OLANGAIANET, KENYA** Young Masai warriors build a wood fire in preparation for cooking a sheep, which they have just killed. *Photograph by James Fisher*

**LAMU ISLAND, KENYA** A family of home cooks makes rice-flour couscous in the common room of their home. *Photograph by James Fisher*

**LOS ANGELES, CALIFORNIA**
A Guatemalan street vendor prepares a *torta* at a food stand that she operates from the back of her truck in a parking lot beneath the freeway. *Photograph by Ariana Lindquist*

**KOSCIUSKO, MISSISSIPPI** A few members of the First Baptist Church show off the bill of fare at their monthly men's prayer breakfast. *Photograph by Penny De Los Santos*

119

PUEBLA, MEXICO A vendor in a night market prepares *chalupas*—fried, crispy corn tortillas—topped with red and green salsas. *Photograph by Penny De Los Santos*

NEW ORLEANS, LOUISIANA Before the lunch rush, cooks at the famed restaurant Commander's Palace gather to hear the rundown of the day's menu. *Photograph by Landon Nordeman*

**NEW YORK, NEW YORK** Cookbook editor and author Judith Jones prepares a dinner for one in her apartment kitchen. *Photograph by David Brabyn/SIPA Press*

**ADDIS ABABA, ETHIOPIA** Bizunesh Sedore, who works as a cook in the home of a local family, makes *injera,* a sourdough flatbread. *Photograph by Barbara Ries*

**CAPE BRETON ISLAND, CANADA** Charlene Murphy, a farmer on this island off the coast of Nova Scotia, prepares a batch of oatcakes for her family.
*Photograph by Landon Nordeman*

**LOS ANGELES, CALIFORNIA** At the Beverly Hills restaurant Spago, chef-owner Wolfgang Puck puts the finishing touches on a dish. *Photograph by Penny De Los Santos*

**BOICEVILLE, NEW YORK** Baker Sonam Norbu holds two sourdough loaves at Bread Alone, the bakery in New York's Hudson Valley where he works. *Photograph by Todd Coleman*

SANTA CRUZ, CALIFORNIA Members of a co-housing community gather in their shared kitchen for a Saturday night dinner. *Photograph by Barbara Ries*

# MEXICO FEEDS ME

**LA YERBABUENA, MEXICO** Marta Rojas at her home, where she makes cheeses using milk from her own herd of cows. *Photograph by Todd Coleman*

MY MOTHER IMMIGRATED to Los Angeles in 1961, but she's never stopped missing the Mexican ranch village of her childhood. Her home state of Zacatecas lies just north of the center of Mexico, and for most of my life she's returned at least once a year to visit her family. This time, I insisted on going with her. I had always heard tales of the place and the people; now, all I could think about was the food. I couldn't wait to eat an authentic *gordita Zacatecana*, a griddled corn cake that puffs up and lets out a hiss of steam when it's ready to be stuffed with cheese, meat, or whatever vegetables are in season. Finally I would taste Aunt Marta's famously pungent raw-milk cheeses at the source. My relatives did not disappoint. It began with our arrival at the home of my aunt Margarita Morales, in the town of Fresnillo, where we found a welcome feast waiting for us; the centerpiece was *rebocado*, a fragrant stew of pork spine and purslane. We quickly fell into a rhythm of visiting a different family member every day, and each visit would mean trying a new dish, like fava bean soup or *asado de bodas*, a rich pork and red chile stew. My cousin Chuyita Sanchez, in the town of San Pablo, made a tart and spicy green mole with tomatillos, jalapeños, and cilantro,

»

**FRESNILLO, MEXICO** Avelina Reyes Castillo and Margarita Morales prepare *gorditas* to be grilled. *Photograph by Todd Coleman*

138

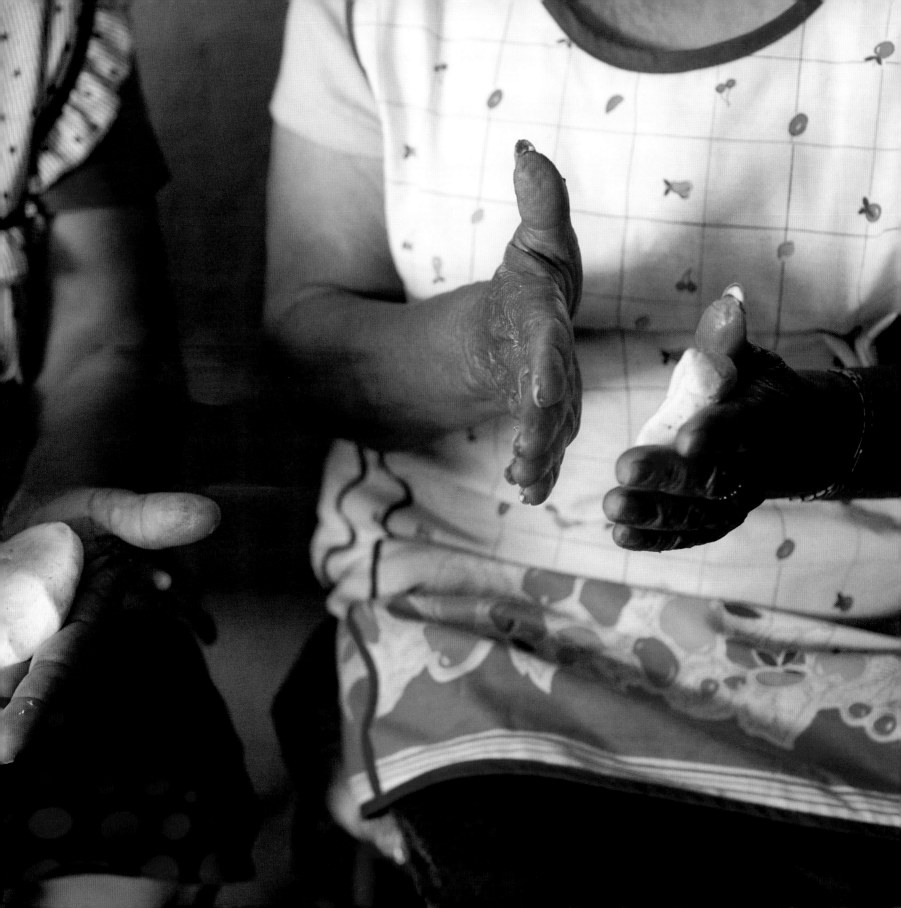

» along with a stewed chicken that she had killed that morning. In San José de Llanetes, a village surrounded by abandoned haciendas, we visited my 86-year-old great-uncle, Guadalupe Rojas. His garden was overflowing with squash blossoms, so we threw together a *guiso* (stew) using the flowers, some onion, sliced jalapeño, and a few tomatoes. Zacatecano ranch life as my mother knew it growing up was often vegetarian by default. She's always reminded me how lucky they were if they had beans to eat, let alone fresh meat or dairy products. To this day, my mother eats a few corn tortillas smeared with a tablespoon of spicy salsa and calls it a meal. Cooking with a *recado*—a flavor base made of pureed tomatoes, onions, garlic, and salt—was the best way of stretching the available vegetables, which might be as sparse as a few ears of corn or as generous as a larder full of chayotes, green beans, potatoes, and peas. On this trip, I stopped taking for granted that resourceful way of cooking, eating, and living. The day I considered myself an adult was the day my aunt Margarita taught me to shape a real *gordita* from fresh *masa*. It was my ancestral food, and it had finally become my own. —*Javier Cabral,* SAVEUR, May 2011

**LA YERBABUENA, MEXICO** Margarita Morales, Marta Rojas, and Maria Rosa Cabral make cheese using fresh *leche de appoyo,* an extra-creamy cows' milk. *Photograph by Todd Coleman*

141

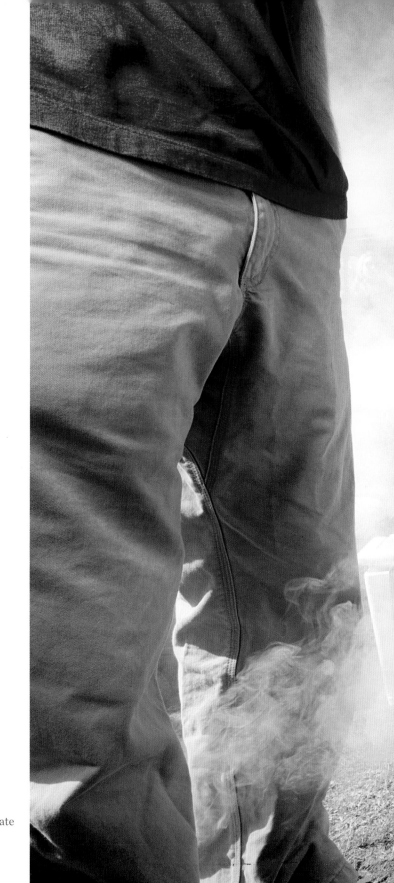

**TALLAHASSEE, FLORIDA** Football fans grill sausages at a tailgate party outside Florida State University's Doak Campbell Stadium. *Photograph by Todd Coleman*

**OLD DELHI, INDIA** Street vendors prepare dough for the Indian flatbread called *naan. Photograph by Penny De Los Santos*

145

**PAPHOS, CYPRUS** Cypriot home cooks, like the woman pictured here, make sweets and pastries using local walnuts (facing page), which are eaten young and green. *Photographs by Penny De Los Santos*

**ROCKLAND, MAINE** A crew member aboard the American Eagle carries a frittata up from the ship's galley. *Photograph by Landon Nordeman*

**NEW YORK, NEW YORK** At the restaurant Park Avenue Winter, chef Craig Koketsu prepares a signature dish, broccoli with Cheetos. *Photograph by Todd Coleman*

**BEIRUT, LEBANON** One evening in the life of a group of Iraqi refugees living in Beirut, from left: Jassim Jaafar (in white) and Ali Shamkhi prepare the foods of their homeland; roommates and friends join them for a home-cooked meal. *Photographs by Penny De Los Santos*

RIGA, LATVIA Home cook Stan-islava Balsa (left) and her daughter Renata prepare lunch. *Photograph by Landon Nordeman*

# LAND OF SPICE

**ISFAHAN, IRAN** Women carrying pots of lamb stew during Ashura, a December holiday when Iranian cooks prepare food to distribute to the poor as well as to neighbors and friends. *Photograph by Ali Farboud*

O N MY FIRST DAY IN TEHRAN, I visited the markets, which were in full bloom with produce from Iran's rich agricultural west. In Tajrish, one of the city's nicest outdoor bazaars, there were bins full of cardamom pods and cinnamon sticks, bottles of rose and other waters distilled from herbs and flowers, and the spice mix called *advieh*, comprising turmeric, cumin, ground coriander, and other spices. I was in the country on a visit to a friend, an architect named Nasrine Faghih, who had moved back to her native Tehran a few years ago. As we wandered through the stalls, Nasrine explained the use of foods that were unfamiliar to me: sour fruit jellies that looked like tiny jewels, used as a relish to flavor fish dishes, and dried orange-blossom petals for tea. We were shopping to cook with her friend Minou Saberi, who joined me later in Nasrine's kitchen to make a *khoresht*, a stew where meat, herbs, and vegetables or fruit slowly simmer until the whole is thick and rich. In Saberi's elegant chicken-and-walnut version, the predominant flavorings of Iranian cooking were front and center: saffron; intensely flavored Omani limes; and sumac, the lemony tasting, crimson-colored berries. The stew had a delectable sweet-tart flavor, one of several fascinating dishes I was served over the course

»

**TEHRAN, IRAN** A waiter serves spiced chicken and tomato kebabs, a popular dish in the city's cafés. *Photograph by Ali Farboud*

158

» of my stay. I was lucky enough, toward the end of my visit, to be in the country the best time to experience Iranians' legendary hospitality: Ashura, a solemn day in December for Shia Muslims that commemorates the martyrdom of the prophet's grandson at the battle of Karbala. I was staying overnight in Isfahan, Iran's third-largest city, for the holiday, when people prepare food to distribute not only to the poor but also to neighbors and friends. The cooks at my hotel prepared a cauldron of *khoresht-e gheimeh* (a stew made with lamb and split peas) that they placed in the hotel's entrance next to a gigantic pot of rice. As neighbors filed in, servers filled containers for them to take home. But even more impressive was the kitchen of the nearby mosque where cooks were preparing enough chicken and lamb *khoresht* to feed a few thousand people. When I returned to Tehran later that evening, I found that Nasrine's neighbor had brought us a plate of cakelike halvah, a dessert that she had made with toasted flour, sugar, and saffron and molded into an elaborate star pattern. As Nasrine and I sat at the table, enjoying the confection, it occurred to me that while none of my meals had been formal or fancy, they had all been delicious and gracious. —*Anissa Helou,* SAVEUR, *March 2012*

**QAZVIN, IRAN** Home cook Fereydoon Abbas Nejad and his family prepare dinner in his kitchen. *Photograph by Ali Farboud*

**JAKARTA, INDONESIA**  A woman prepares breakfast in the indoor-outdoor kitchen of her home. *Photograph by James Oseland*

163

**PORTLAND, OREGON** Baker Mary Casanave Sheridan at The Honey Pot, a food cart that serves pies and other desserts. *Photograph by Todd Coleman*

KATONAH, NEW YORK After checking a recipe (above), artist and cookbook author Edward Giobbi prepares lunch in the kitchen of the home he has lived in for 50 years.
*Photographs by André Baranowski*

**NOTO, ITALY** Chef Corrado Assenza stands outside his pastry shop, Caffè Sicilia. *Photograph by Landon Nordeman*

**SOURE, BRAZIL** Jerônima Brito (left) and her sister Ângela in their kitchen on Marajó Island in northern Brazil. *Photograph by James Oseland*

IZGARA KÖFTE

PIYAZ

SPECIAL KASAPLI KÖFTE 2.50

KÖFTE ARASI KÖFTE 4.00

ÇORBA 2.00

SÜTLÜ TATLILAR

ATALAR 2.50

ATALAR 2.50

BARDAK SU 0.50

ŞİŞE SU 0.75

3.00 YTL

2.00 YTL

2.50 YTL

2.50 YTL

2.50 YTL

**BUL, TURKEY** Fragrant spiced
cook over hardwood charcoal
of the city's many kebab shops.
*raph by Landon Nordeman*

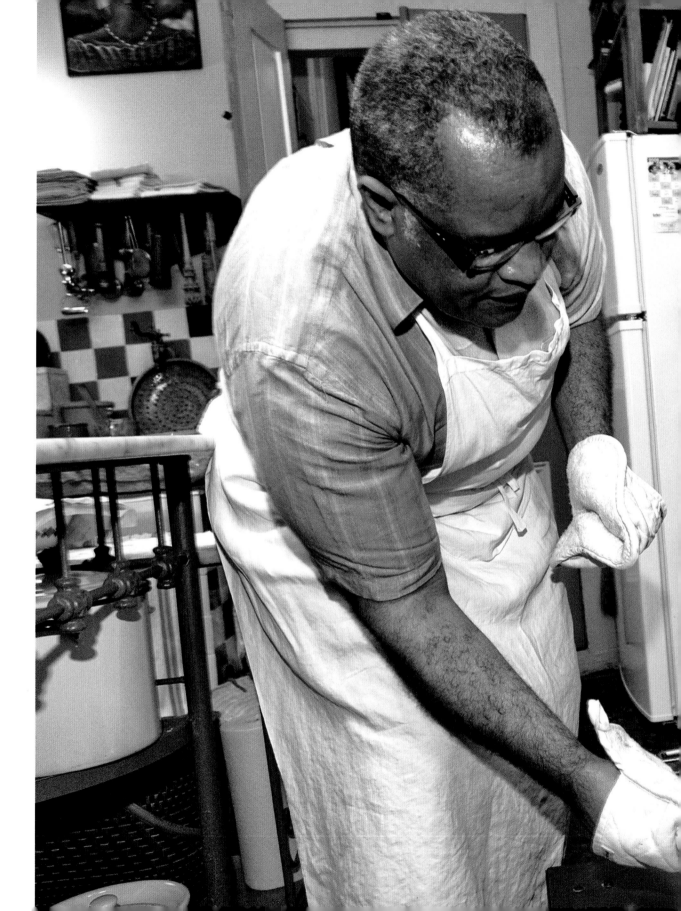

**NEW ORLEANS, LOUISIANA** Home cook Kerry Moody pulls yeast rolls out of the oven. *Photograph by Rebecca McAlpin*

PHUNG HIEP, VIETNAM At a floating market on the Mekong River, a vendor sells sodas, snacks, and coffee from her boat. *Photograph by Penny De Los Santos*

# THE GIVING EARTH

**MIKLÓSVÁR, ROMANIA** Agnes Elek, a cook at a guesthouse in the Transylvania region, prepares dinner. *Photograph by Landon Nordeman*

THE SAXON VILLAGE OF MEŞENDORF, in Transylvania, looked like a stage set from Chaucer's *Canterbury Tales.* We were there to visit the farm of Mariana and Gheorghe Bardas. Beyond the tattered Roma settlement on the edge of town, geese and ducks wandered the tidy green swards on the village's broad main street, which was shaded by pear, chestnut, and walnut trees. Past a gate in a wall just wide enough for a hay cart, the sweet smell of wood smoke filled the air of the Bardas' narrow plot. Mariana Bardas showed off her henhouse, pigpen, and vegetable garden planted with potatoes, beans, peppers, tomatoes, cabbage, carrots, corn, and onions. Then she swept the ashes from her wood-burning oven with green elder switches and loaded it with six big rounds of wheat-flour dough, enough to feed her family for two weeks. I was fascinated to see that she deliberately let the loaves bake past the point when another baker in another place might have considered them burned. When the bread emerged jet black an hour later, she let it cool and then beat each loaf with a wooden rolling pin to remove the char and reveal a thick nut-brown crust. On special occasions, she told us, to achieve a softer crust, she'd wrap the dough with cabbage leaves before baking.

»

**MIKLÓSVÁR, ROMANIA** A kitchen in a home on a Transylvanian estate. *Photograph by Landon Nordeman*

»

Over the next few days, as we explored Biertan, Copșa Mare, Mălăncrav, and other Saxon settlements, taking pleasure in the sentient landscape, wandering the villages, and eating tasty farm food, I couldn't help but wonder if Transylvania's sweet hospitality and fragile beauty will survive the changes that modernity and increased connection to the outside world are sure to bring. Then I met Gerda Gherghiceanu, who runs a simple restaurant in her farmhouse in Viscri, a typically Saxon village with a fortified church. One of the last Saxons in the village, Gherghiceanu's pride is serving echt Saxon dishes. Lunch in late June ran to a soup of deeply flavored rooster stock with runner beans, tomatoes, and carrots; a rich pork-and-potato stew fragrant with fresh marjoram; cabbage salad; and freshly baked almond cake topped with just-picked apricots. After Gherghiceanu shooed away our compliments, I changed the subject. Why had she stayed behind when so many other Saxons had left Transylvania? "I've traveled, you know. My brother lives in Germany, and he has a big house and a fancy car, but we have a much, much better life here," she said with a grin. "Best of all," she added, "my children know it, too." —*Alexander Lobrano,* SAVEUR, *March 2012*

**VISCRI, ROMANIA** Gerda Gherghiceanu (center) looks on as a couple enjoys lunch at her farmhouse restaurant in Transylvania. *Photograph by Landon Nordeman*

Special

1 Chop Beef          3.00
        OR
2 Chop Beef for      5.00

**TAYLOR, TEXAS** Owner and pitmaster
Vencil Mares relaxes behind the bar of
his barbecue restaurant, Taylor Cafe.
*Photograph by O. Rufus Lovett*

**MUMBAI, INDIA** A cook in a restaurant halves almonds in the late afternoon.
*Photograph by Ariana Lindquist*

**LAS VEGAS, NEVADA** Richard Bunker (center), a descendant of some of Nevada's earliest Mormon pioneers, has lunch with his son Richard (left) and grandson Tristan. *Photograph by Todd Coleman*

**LOS ANGELES, CALIFORNIA** A cook at Angeli Caffe, a one-time restaurant in West Hollywood, tosses dough for a pizza. *Photograph by Ariana Lindquist*

**OULX, ITALY** At left, Lucia Gros Corradin, a home cook in the Italian Alps, in her kitchen; at right, Corradin and her daughter, Roberta, linger over dessert. *Photographs by Penny De Los Santos*

**SINGAPORE** Hong Suen Wong waits at the kitchen table while her mother, Mei Teck Wong, in the background, prepares more dishes. *Photograph by James Oseland*

**BOLOGNA, ITALY** A pasta maker untangles strands of freshly rolled and cut tagliatelle. *Photograph by Landon Nordeman*

JERUSALEM, ISRAEL Two cooks stand at the ready for the evening crowds at Sima, a restaurant that specializes in grilled meat. *Photograph by Penny De Los Santos*

**SUZHOU, CHINA** Scenes from a family lunch, from left: home cook Yan Zaijun in her apartment with her granddaughter; stir-fried shrimp with scallions; setting the table for lunch; the Yan family sits down to the meal. *Photograph by Ariana Lindquist*

**KINGSTON, JAMAICA** At left, a cook prepares the fire at Scotchies, a jerk chicken restaurant on the west side of town; at right, brothers Dameko and Ricky Holland take a break from the morning rush at their downtown food stall, Charley Mattrass Porridge Center. *Photographs by Landon Nordeman*

**MONTOGGIO, ITALY** Enrichetta Truccho, a home cook, rolls out dough for lasagne while her son, Sergio Rossi, looks on. *Photograph by Penny De Los Santos*

**NEW YORK, NEW YORK** A counterman carves pastrami at Katz's Delicatessen on Manhattan's Lower East Side. *Photograph by Landon Nordeman*

**CHICAGO, ILLINOIS** Grant Achatz, chef-owner of the restaurant Alinea, with his Heidolph Brinkmann Laborota 20 Rotary Evaporator, one of the many high-tech tools he uses in his kitchen. *Photograph by Beth Rooney*

GUBBIO, ITALY The Italian chef
Lidia Bastianich shows four of her
grandchildren how to knead dough.
*Photograph by Penny De Los Santos*

**HATAY, TURKEY** A baker makes *kunefe,* a traditional sweet consisting of vermicelli-like strands of pastry, by pouring streams of thin batter onto a hot, rotating plate. *Photograph by Todd Coleman*

**KINGSTON, JAMAICA** Employees at Susie's Bakery and Coffee Bar, at the tail end of a busy brunch shift. *Photograph by Landon Nordeman*

**HUNTSVILLE, TEXAS** A Friday morning at the barbecue pit run by New Zion Missionary Baptist Church, from left: the firebox, filled with burning oak wood, that fuels the metal drum smoker; Clayton "Smitty" Smith and pitmaster Robert Polk take a break from tending the flames. *Photographs by Penny De Los Santos*

**LOS ANGELES, CALIFORNIA** At La Abeja, a Mexican-American restaurant, moments of quiet between the breakfast and lunch rushes, from left: a line cook takes a break; a section of the restaurant reserved as a place for staff to sit and have a meal before returning to the kitchen. *Photograph by Penny De Los Santos*

Baked eggs with chanterelles (page 226). *Photograph by Landon Nordeman*

# RECIPES

## MAIN DISHES

Baked Eggs with Chanterelles
**PARIS, FRANCE**

Pork with Apples
and Cider Cream Sauce
**VISCRI, ROMANIA**

Braised Chicken with
Garlic and Peppers
**CHARLESTON, SOUTH CAROLINA**

Stuffed Cabbage Rolls
**BROOKLYN, NEW YORK**

Stir-Fried Beef and
Green Beans
**BEIJING, CHINA**

Stuffed Eggplant
**PIGADI, GREECE**

Brazilian Fish with
Shrimp Sauce
**SOURE, BRAZIL**

Red Chile Enchiladas
**ZACATECAS, MEXICO**

Smokestack's Barbecued
Chicken Wings
**KANSAS CITY, MISSOURI**

Fish Croquettes in Spiced
Tomato Sauce
**BROOKLYN, NEW YORK**

Wild Greens with
Fried Eggs
**EPIRUS, GREECE**

Steak Tartare
**PARIS, FRANCE**

Steak with Melted
Mozzarella
**SOURE, BRAZIL**

Grilled Whole Fish
with Tamarind
**LAMU ISLAND, KENYA**

Pasta with Sardines
**SICILY, ITALY**

Braised "Lion's Head"
Meatballs with Napa Cabbage
**LAS VEGAS, NEVADA**

## SIDE DISHES

Avocado-Mango Salad
**DAKAR, SENEGAL**

Stewed Green Beans
**CHARLESTON, SOUTH CAROLINA**

Broccoli with Cheetos
**NEW YORK, NEW YORK**

Pickled Radishes
and Green Onion
**LAS VEGAS, NEVADA**

Buttermilk Biscuits
**KOSCIUSKO, MISSISSIPPI**

Dry-Cured Olives with
Rosemary and Orange
**SICILY, ITALY**

Cheese and Bread Soup
**OULX, ITALY**

Fennel and Herb
Phyllo Pastries
**LOS ANGELES, CALIFORNIA**

Umbrian Vegetable Soup
**GUBBIO, ITALY**

Indian Flatbread
**AHMEDABAD, INDIA**

New Orleans Oyster Stew
**NEW ORLEANS, LOUSIANA**

Chickpeas with
Pickled Mango
**PORTLAND, OREGON**

Stewed Rutabagas
**CHARLESTON, SOUTH CAROLINA**

Layered Herring Salad
**RIGA, LATVIA**

Bistro French Fries
**PARIS, FRANCE**

Ricotta Crostini with Black
Olives, Lemon Zest, and Mint
**CALABRIA, ITALY**

Ricotta Crostini with
Cherry Tomatoes
**CALABRIA, ITALY**

Ricotta Crostini with
Chestnut Honey
**CALABRIA, ITALY**

Ricotta Crostini
with Soppressata
**CALABRIA, ITALY**

Cape Breton Potato Salad
**CAPE BRETON ISLAND, CANADA**

Yogurt and Cucumber
**QAZVIN, IRAN**

Gujarati Cabbage
**AHMEDABAD, INDIA**

Rice and Beans
**SOURE, BRAZIL**

Black-Eyed Pea Salad
**DAKAR, SENEGAL**

Feta Tart
**VISSANI, GREECE**

## DESSERTS

Ricotta and Coffee Mousse
**CALABRIA, ITALY**

Waffle Cones Filled with
Sweet Cheese and Berries
**LAUNKALNE, LATVIA**

Brazilian Banana
Pudding
**SOURE, BRAZIL**

Apricot Cake
**VISCRI, ROMANIA**

Pineapple Upside-Down Cake
**HUMBOLDT COUNTY, CALIFORNIA**

Amadeus Cookies,
**VIENNA, AUSTRIA**

Strawberry Cake
**CHARLESTON, SOUTH CAROLINA**

Sweet Porridge with
Raisins and Almonds
**AHMEDABAD, INDIA**

# MAIN DISHES

### Baked Eggs with Chanterelles

*(Oeufs Cocotte aux Girolles)*

SERVES 4

Garlic is used in three different ways—sautéed, as a confit, and rubbed on toast—to build depth of flavor in this French bistro classic of eggs, spinach, and mushrooms gently cooked in a cream bath (pictured on page 224).

- $3/4$ cup extra-virgin olive oil
- 4 cloves garlic
- 4 tbsp. unsalted butter
- 8 oz. spinach, stemmed
  Kosher salt and freshly ground black pepper, to taste
- 8 oz. chanterelle or cremini mushrooms, quartered
- $1/3$ cup heavy cream
- 4 eggs
- 1 baguette, cut on the diagonal into thick slices

1 Make the garlic confit: Heat oil in a 1-qt. saucepan over medium-low heat. Add 2 cloves garlic and cook, stirring occasionally, until garlic is tender, 15–20 minutes. Using a slotted spoon, transfer garlic to a cutting board; let cool. Thinly slice garlic confit lengthwise. (Reserve garlic-flavored oil for another use, such as making vinaigrette or poaching fish.)

2 Melt 2 tbsp. butter in a 12" skillet over medium heat until foamy. Add spinach and cook, stirring occasionally, until tender, about 6 minutes. Season with salt and pepper. Transfer spinach to a tea towel and wipe out skillet. Gather up ends of towel and squeeze out excess liquid; set spinach aside.

3 Melt remaining butter in skillet over medium heat. Add 1 clove garlic and the mushrooms, season with salt and pepper, and cook, stirring occasionally, for 5 minutes. Add heavy cream and cook 5 minutes more. Remove pan from heat, cover, and let mushrooms steep for 15 minutes. Discard garlic.

4 Heat oven to 400°. Divide the spinach and mushrooms between four 6-oz. ramekins. Add reserved slices of garlic confit. Crack 1 egg into each ramekin. Transfer ramekins to a 9" x 13" baking pan and pour enough boiling water into pan to come halfway up the side of the ramekins. Cover pan with aluminum foil and transfer to oven; cook until whites are set and yolks are still runny, about 10 minutes. Meanwhile, toast the baguette slices and rub them with the remaining garlic clove. To serve, divide ramekins and slices of toasted baguettes between 4 plates, and season eggs with salt and pepper.

### Pork with Apples and Cider Cream Sauce

*(Székelyalmás)*

SERVES 6

Gerda Ghergiceanu (page 182) serves this dish of tender, juicy pork loin in a tart and creamy sauce at her farmhouse restaurant in rural Transylvania.

- $1/3$ cup olive oil
- 4 tbsp. unsalted butter
- $1\,1/2$ lb. pork loin, cut into $1/4$"-thick slices
  Kosher salt and freshly ground black pepper, to taste
- $1/2$ cup flour
- 3 tart apples, such as Granny Smith, peeled, cored, and cut into 8 wedges each
- 3 cloves garlic, finely chopped
- 1 large yellow onion, finely chopped
- $1/2$ red Holland chile, stemmed, seeded, and minced
- $1\,1/2$ cups regular or hard apple cider
- 1 cup chicken stock
- $1/2$ cup heavy cream
- $1/4$ cup Dijon mustard
- 1 tbsp. finely chopped marjoram
- 1 tbsp. finely chopped parsley
  Cooked white rice, for serving

1 Heat 2 tbsp. each oil and butter in a 12" skillet over medium-high heat. Season pork on both sides with salt and pepper, and dredge half the pieces in flour; add to skillet, and cook, turning once, until lightly browned on both sides, about 1 minute. Transfer to a plate and set aside.

2 Repeat with 2 tbsp. oil, remaining butter, and remaining pork and flour. Return skillet to heat and add remaining oil. Add apples, garlic, onion, and chile, and cook, stirring occasionally, until soft, about 3 minutes. Add cider and cook until reduced by half, about 5 minutes. Add stock, cream, and mustard, and bring to a boil; return pork to skillet, and add marjoram. Reduce heat to medium, and simmer until pork is cooked through and sauce has thickened, about 3 minutes. Season with salt and pepper, and sprinkle with parsley; serve with rice.

### Braised Chicken with Garlic and Peppers

SERVES 8

This slow-braised chicken (pictured on page 229) is a soul food staple at Charleston, South Carolina, restaurants like Martha Lou's Kitchen (page 15).

- 8 whole chicken legs
  Kosher salt, freshly ground black pepper, and paprika, to taste
- $1/4$ cup canola oil
- 4 cloves garlic, roughly chopped
- 2 large green bell peppers, stemmed, seeded, and cut into $1/2$"-thick strips
- 2 large yellow onions, halved lengthwise and cut into $1/2$"-thick slices
- $1/4$ cup tomato paste
- 1 cup chicken stock

1 Heat oven to 400°. Season chicken liberally with salt, pepper, and paprika. Heat oil in an 8-qt. saucepan over medium-high heat. Working in batches, add chicken, skin side down, and cook until skin is golden brown,

Clockwise from top left: braised chicken with garlic and peppers (page 226); stuffed cabbage rolls; stir-fried beef and green beans; stuffed eggplant.

about 6 minutes. Reserve oil and arrange chicken in a large roasting pan in a single layer, skin side up, and set aside.

**2** Return saucepan to heat and add garlic, peppers, and onions; cook, stirring, until vegetables begin to soften, about 8 minutes. Stir in tomato paste; cook for 1 minute. Add chicken stock; scrape browned bits off bottom of pan and mix. Pour vegetables and stock around chicken, and bake until chicken is browned and cooked through, about 1 hour.

## Stuffed Cabbage Rolls

*(Holishkes)*

SERVES 6–8

Oven-braised until tender, these beef-stuffed cabbage rolls in tomato sauce are served for the Sukkot holiday in the Lubavitch Jewish community of Brooklyn, New York (page 88).

    Kosher salt, to taste
1  large head cabbage, cored
2  tbsp. canola oil
2  medium yellow onions, thinly sliced, plus 1/2 cup finely grated
2  ribs celery, finely chopped
    Freshly ground black pepper, to taste
1/4  cup tomato paste
1/3  cup raisins
1/4  cup honey
1/4  cup fresh lemon juice
1  32-oz. can whole peeled tomatoes with juice, puréed
1  lb. ground chuck

1/4  cup uncooked long-grain white rice, soaked in hot water for 10 minutes, drained
3  tbsp. beef stock
1  tsp. paprika
1/4  tsp. cayenne
1  egg, lightly beaten

**1** Bring a large pot of salted water to a boil over high heat; add cabbage, and cook, pulling off each outer leaf with tongs as it becomes tender, about 2 minutes per leaf. Transfer leaves to a baking sheet and continue until you have 20 leaves.

**2** Heat oil in a 6-qt. saucepan over medium-high heat; add sliced onions and celery, season with salt and pepper, and cook, stirring, until lightly caramelized, about 15 minutes. Add tomato paste, and cook, stirring, until lightly caramelized, about 2 minutes. Add raisins, honey, juice, and tomatoes, and bring to a boil; reduce heat to medium-low, and cook, partially covered, until reduced, about 30 minutes.

**3** Heat oven to 350°. Combine grated onion, chuck, rice, stock, paprika, cayenne, egg, and salt and pepper in a bowl. Place 2 tbsp. beef mixture in center of each cabbage leaf, fold sides over filling, and then roll up. Transfer rolls, seam side down, to a 9″ × 13″ glass baking dish. Pour tomato sauce over rolls; bake until filling is cooked through, about 45 minutes.

## Stir-Fried Beef and Green Beans

*(Sijidou Chao Niurou)*

SERVES 2–4

Quick-cooking, flavorful stir-fries like this one are a standby among cooks in Beijing, like Deng Haiyan (page 187).

5  oz. top sirloin beef, cut across the grain into 1/4″-thick slices
2 1/2  tsp. soy sauce
1 1/2  tsp. rice cooking wine
1 1/2  tsp. cornstarch
1 1/2  tsp. freshly ground black pepper
8  oz. large green beans, trimmed and cut diagonally into 1/4″ slices
1  tbsp. peanut oil
1  2″-piece ginger, minced
2  cloves garlic, thinly sliced lengthwise
    Kosher salt, to taste

**1** Combine beef slices, 1 1/2 tsp. soy sauce, cooking wine, cornstarch, and pepper in a medium bowl and toss to combine; set aside. Bring a small pot of water to a boil, and add beans; cook until crisp-tender, about 2 minutes. Drain and set aside to cool.

**2** Heat a 14″ flat-bottomed wok or skillet over high heat until wok begins to smoke. Add oil around edge of wok, and then add ginger; cook, stirring constantly, until fragrant, about 20 seconds. Add beef slices in a single layer, and cook, turning once, until browned, about 3 minutes.

**3** Add remaining soy sauce and the garlic, and cook, stirring constantly, until fragrant, about 1 minute. Add beans, and cook, stirring often, until warmed through, about 4 minutes. Season with salt and transfer to a serving dish or bowls; serve immediately.

## Stuffed Eggplant

*(Papoutsakia)*

SERVES 6

On the Peloponnese peninsula of southern Greece (page 92), eggplants, an abundant local crop, are stuffed with ground beef and tomatoes and topped with a cheesy béchamel sauce to make this dish.

6  small eggplants (1 lb. each)
3/4  cup extra-virgin olive oil
7  cloves garlic, minced
1  medium yellow onion, minced
12  oz. ground beef, pork, or lamb
    Kosher salt and freshly ground black pepper, to taste
2  cups crushed tomatoes
3/4  cup dry red wine
2  tbsp. dried oregano
1/4  tsp. ground cinnamon
1/8  tsp. ground cloves
4  tbsp. unsalted butter
1/2  cup flour
2  cups milk
1 1/2  cups finely grated Parmesan cheese
2  egg yolks
    Pinch of freshly grated nutmeg, to taste

From left: Brazilian fish with shrimp sauce and fried plantains; red chile enchiladas (page 234).

1 Cut each eggplant in half lengthwise and, using a spoon, scoop out most of the flesh, leaving a ½"-thick eggplant shell. Coarsely chop the scooped-out eggplant flesh and set aside. Heat ¼ cup oil in a 12" skillet over medium-high heat. Working in 2 batches, add eggplant shells and cook, turning once, until browned and just wilted, about 5 minutes. Transfer eggplant shells to paper towels; set aside. Discard oil and wipe out skillet.

2 Heat ¼ cup oil in the skillet over medium-high heat; add garlic and onion, and cook, stirring often, until soft, about 5 minutes. Add meat, breaking it into small pieces with a wooden spoon, and season with salt and pepper; cook, stirring occasionally, until browned, about 5 minutes. Stir in reserved eggplant flesh, tomatoes, wine, oregano, cinnamon, and cloves; season with salt and pepper and bring to a simmer. Cook, stirring occasionally, until sauce has thickened, about 45 minutes. Remove pan from heat, and set meat sauce aside.

3 Heat butter in a 4-qt. saucepan over medium-high heat. Add flour and cook, whisking constantly, until smooth and slightly toasted, 1–2 minutes. Add milk; cook, whisking often, until sauce coats the back of a spoon, 8–10 minutes. Remove from heat, add ¾ cup cheese and egg yolks;

season with salt, pepper, and nutmeg. Stir béchamel until smooth; set aside.

4 Heat oven to 350°. Put eggplant shells, cut side up, on a rimmed baking sheet. Sprinkle shells with half the remaining cheese and fill each with some of the reserved meat sauce. Spoon béchamel over top, and sprinkle with remaining cheese. Bake until eggplants are tender, about 20 minutes. Increase heat to broil, and cook until béchamel is golden brown and bubbly, about 5 minutes more.

## Brazilian Fish with Shrimp Sauce

*(Filhote com Molho de Camarões e Bananas)*

SERVES 6

Jerônima Brito (pictured on page 170), a rancher on Marajó Island in northern Brazil, shared her recipe for this seafood dish with a spicy shrimp sauce and a garnish of sweet fried plantains.

3½ lb. bone-in, skin-on red snapper steaks (about 5)
    Kosher salt and freshly ground black pepper, to taste
⅓ cup olive oil
¼ cup minced cilantro
¼ cup minced Thai or lemon basil
1 tbsp. minced pickled chiles, such as jalapeños (optional)
2 tsp. ground annatto seed (optional)
1 lb. medium shrimp, peeled, deveined, and roughly chopped
2 tbsp. fresh lime juice

231

From left: Smokestack's barbecued chicken wings (page 234); wild greens with fried eggs (page 235).

232

1 small yellow onion,
  finely chopped
1 tbsp. minced garlic
½ Italian or cubanelle pepper,
  stemmed, seeded, and finely
  chopped
3 plum tomatoes, cored
  and finely chopped
1 cup fish or vegetable stock
  Canola oil, for frying
1 ripe plantain, peeled and
  cut into ¼"-thick slices

1 Place fish in a large baking dish and
  season with salt and pepper. Rub
with ¼ cup olive oil, 2 tbsp. cilantro,
2 tbsp. basil, the chiles, and 1 tsp. annatto; let marinate at room temperature
for 20 minutes. Meanwhile, in a small
bowl, toss together shrimp and lime
juice; marinate for at least 10 minutes.

2 Heat a 12" skillet over medium-
  high heat. Working in batches,
add fish and marinade, and cook, turning once, until cooked through, about
12 minutes. Transfer fish to a serving
platter and keep warm.

3 Return skillet with marinade to
  heat, and add remaining olive oil
and onions; cook, stirring, until soft,
about 4 minutes. Add garlic and pepper,
and cook, stirring, until soft, about
3 minutes. Add tomatoes, and cook
until liquid evaporates and mixture is
lightly caramelized, about 12 minutes.
Add remaining annatto, reserved shrimp
with juice, and stock; cook, stirring,
until shrimp are just cooked through,

about 2 minutes. Stir in remaining
cilantro and basil, and season with salt
and pepper; pour sauce over fish.

4 Meanwhile, pour canola oil to a
  depth of 1" in a 12" skillet and heat
over medium-high heat. Add plantains,
and fry, turning once, until browned
and tender, about 5 minutes. Transfer
to paper towels to drain, and season
with salt. Serve with fish.

## Red Chile Enchiladas
MAKES 12
We got this recipe for enchiladas
drenched in a rich sauce made with
fruity dried chiles and chocolate
(pictured on page 231) from Marta
Rojas, a home cook and dairy farmer
in Zacatecas, Mexico (page 140).

8 dried New Mexico chiles,
  stemmed and seeded
1 oz. Mexican chocolate, such
  as Ibarra, roughly chopped
½ tsp. dried oregano
¼ tsp. ground cinnamon
4 saltine crackers, or 2½ tbsp.
  bread crumbs
1 clove garlic
1 whole clove
1 tbsp. canola oil, plus more for frying
  Kosher salt, to taste
2 cups crumbled queso añejo
  or feta, plus more to garnish
½ small yellow onion, minced
12 corn tortillas
  Thinly sliced white onion rings,
  to garnish

1 Make the red chile sauce: Heat
  chiles in a 12" skillet over high
heat, and cook, turning as needed,
until toasted, about 5 minutes. Transfer chiles to a blender with chocolate,
oregano, cinnamon, crackers, garlic,
clove, and 1½ cups boiling water,
and let sit for 5 minutes. Purée until
smooth, and then pour sauce through
a fine strainer into a bowl. Heat 1 tbsp.
oil in a 2-qt. saucepan over medium-
high heat, and add chile sauce; cook,
stirring often, until reduced and
thickened, about 6 minutes. Season
with salt and set aside.

2 To assemble the enchiladas,
  combine the queso añejo and onion
in a small bowl and set aside. Pour oil
to a depth of 2" in a 6-qt. Dutch oven
and heat over medium-high heat until
a deep-fry thermometer reads 350°.
Using tongs, grasp all the tortillas in
a stack and submerge in oil, swirling
in oil until slightly fried and pliable,
about 15 seconds. (The surface of the
tortillas should puff up in tiny pockets
in several places.) Remove from oil and
set aside on a plate to cool. (Alternatively,
you may wrap the tortillas in a damp
towel and briefly microwave until
warm.) Working in batches, dip each
tortilla in chile sauce until completely
coated. Transfer to a plate and top
with 3 tbsp. cheese filling; roll up like
a cigar and sprinkle with more cheese.
Arrange on a platter and top with onion
rings. Serve with rice and beans.

## Smokestack's Barbecued Chicken Wings
SERVES 6–8
Barbecue can be anything from the
pulled pork and ribs served in Arkansas,
South Carolina, and other parts of the
American South (pages 26 to 33) to
these crisp-charred, butter-bathed
chicken wings (pictured on page 232)
from Smokestack BBQ in Kansas
City, Missouri.

1 tbsp. kosher salt
2¼ tsp. sweet paprika
1½ tsp. garlic powder
1½ tsp. onion powder
1½ tsp. dried thyme
1½ tsp. dried oregano
¾ tsp. ground black pepper
¾ tsp. ground white pepper
½ tsp. dried sage
½ tsp. cayenne
2½ lb. chicken wings
16 tbsp. unsalted butter, melted
½ cup mild hot sauce
¼ cup Old Bay seasoning
  Juice of 1 lemon
  Handful of oak wood chunks,
  soaked in water for 10 minutes

1 In a bowl, whisk together salt,
  paprika, garlic and onion powders,
thyme, oregano, both peppers, sage,
and cayenne. Toss wings with spices
in bowl; cover and chill 4 hours.

2 Meanwhile, whisk together butter,
  hot sauce, Old Bay, and lemon juice
in a large bowl, then pour half the sauce
into another large bowl. Set both aside.

**3** Build a medium-hot fire in a charcoal grill. Place damp oak wood chunks directly on coals and replace grill grate. Cover grill and let heat for 10 minutes. Place chicken wings on grill grate. Maintaining a temperature of 225°–250° (replenish fire with unlit coals, as needed, to maintain temperature) cook, covered, turning once, for 20 minutes. Toss chicken wings in half the sauce, return to grill, and cook until well browned and tender, about 25 minutes.

**4** To serve, toss chicken wings in remaining bowl of sauce, and serve immediately.

## Fish Croquettes in Spiced Tomato Sauce
*(Blehat)*
SERVES 4

The Lubavitch Jewish community in Brooklyn, New York (page 88), celebrates the Sukkot holiday with festive foods like these savory fish croquettes in a cumin-spiced tomato sauce (pictured on page 255).

- 1 lb. cod or haddock, finely chopped in a food processor
- 1/2 cup matzo meal
- 1/4 cup finely chopped parsley
- 1 tsp. ground cumin
- 1/2 tsp. ground coriander
- 1/4 tsp. ground ginger
- 5 cloves garlic, finely chopped
- 1 egg white, lightly beaten

   Kosher salt and freshly ground black pepper, to taste
- 2 tbsp. canola oil
- 3 tbsp. tomato paste
- 2 cups fish or vegetable stock
- 1 cup whole, peeled canned tomatoes with juice, crushed
- 1 tsp. sugar, plus more to taste
- 1/2 tsp. cayenne
- 1/4 tsp. crushed red chile flakes
- 1/4 tsp. ground allspice

**1** Stir together fish, matzo meal, 3 tbsp. parsley, cumin, coriander, ginger, 2 cloves garlic, egg white, and salt and pepper in a bowl. Form into thirty-two 1/2-oz. balls; chill.

**2** Heat oil in a 4-qt. saucepan over medium-high heat. Add remaining garlic; cook until fragrant, about 45 seconds. Add tomato paste; cook, stirring, until caramelized, about 3 minutes. Add stock, tomatoes, sugar, cayenne, chile flakes, allspice, and salt and pepper; bring to a boil. Add fish balls, reduce heat to medium-low, and cook until cooked through, about 20 minutes. Sprinkle with remaining parsley.

## Wild Greens with Fried Eggs
*(Horta me Avga Tiganita)*
SERVES 6

This dish from Epirus, Greece (page 36), combines luscious fried eggs with pleasingly bitter greens (pictured on page 233).

- 1 1/4 cups extra-virgin olive oil
- 10 scallions, minced
- 1 3/4 lbs. mixed greens, such as nettles, lamb's-quarter, spinach, Swiss chard, radicchio, and arugula, washed and minced
- 1 cup chopped flat-leaf parsley
- 1 cup chopped mint leaves
- 1/2 cup chopped fennel fronds
- 6 cloves garlic, minced
   Kosher salt and freshly ground black pepper, to taste
- 6 eggs

**1** Heat 1/2 cup oil in a 5-qt. pot over medium-high heat. Add scallions, and cook for 4 minutes. Add greens, parsley, mint, fennel, garlic, and 1/2 cup water; season with salt and pepper. Cook, stirring, until greens are tender, 18–20 minutes. Remove from heat.

**2** Heat remaining oil in a 12" skillet over medium-high heat. Working in two batches, crack eggs into skillet; cook, constantly spooning oil over yolks, until yolks are just set, about 2 minutes. Using a slotted spoon, transfer eggs to a plate. Divide greens between plates, and top each with a fried egg.

## Steak Tartare
*(Tartare de Filet de Boeuf)*
SERVES 2

At Le Bistrot Paul Bert in Paris, France, they make this classic tartare (pictured on page 91) studded with diced red onion and salty capers. Serve with

Dijon mustard and bistro French fries (page 250).

- 8 oz. trimmed center-cut beef tenderloin
- 3 tbsp. extra-virgin olive oil, plus more to taste
- 1 egg yolk
- 3 tbsp. salt-packed capers, soaked in water, rinsed, and drained
- 2 tbsp. minced flat-leaf parsley
- 1 small red onion, minced
- 1 red thai chile, stemmed, seeded, and minced
   Kosher salt and freshly ground black pepper, to taste
   Sherry vinegar, to taste
   Dijon mustard, for serving

**1** Chill beef in freezer for 45 minutes to firm it. Transfer beef to cutting board and, using a very sharp knife, cut beef lengthwise into 1/8"-thick slices. Julienne each slice, and cut each julienne crosswise to finely mince beef. Transfer beef to a bowl, cover, and refrigerate.

**2** Meanwhile, drizzle oil into a medium bowl and stir in egg yolk. Add capers, parsley, onion, and chiles; season with salt and pepper. Fold in reserved minced beef, and season to taste with salt, pepper, and oil, if you like, along with a few drops of vinegar. Mound tartare on 2 chilled serving plates.

From left: steak with melted mozzarella; grilled whole fish with tamarind.

## Steak with Melted Mozzarella

*(Filé Marajoara)*

SERVES 4

This luscious combination of soft cheese melted over tender filet mignon is a specialty of Marajó Island in northern Brazil (page 170).

- 4  8-oz. filet mignon steaks
  Kosher salt and freshly ground black pepper, to taste
- ¼  cup olive oil
- 3  tbsp. minced cilantro
- 7  cloves garlic, mashed into a paste with 1 tsp. kosher salt
  Canola oil, for frying
- 2  russet potatoes, peeled and very thinly sliced on a mandoline
- 1  8-oz. ball fresh mozzarella, cut into 4 large slices

1 Season steaks with salt and pepper in a large baking dish. Add oil, cilantro, and garlic, and rub all over steaks; let marinate at room temperature for 30 minutes. Meanwhile, pour oil to a depth of 2" in a 6-qt. Dutch oven, and heat over medium-high heat until a deep-fry thermometer registers 375°. Place potatoes in a colander, and rinse under cold water for 1 minute. Drain potatoes, and transfer to paper towels to dry thoroughly. Working in batches, fry potatoes until light golden brown and crisp, about 2 minutes. Using a slotted spoon, transfer potatoes to paper towels to drain, and season with salt.

2 Heat a 12" skillet over high heat. Add steaks to pan, and cook until browned on bottom, about 3 minutes. Flip steaks, and cook for 1 minute. Place 1 piece mozzarella over each steak and cover skillet; cook until cheese is melted and steaks are cooked to medium-rare, about 2 minutes. Serve with fried potatoes.

## Grilled Whole Fish with Tamarind

*(Samaki Wa Kupaka)*

SERVES 2–4

Basted in a fruity sauce of coconut and tamarind, this grilled fish epitomizes the brightly flavored, seafood-rich cuisine found on the coast of Kenya, in East Africa (page 115).

- 1  2–3-lb. whole fish, such as red snapper, porgy, or striped bass, cleaned
  Kosher salt and freshly ground black pepper, to taste
- 6  cloves garlic, minced
- 2  green Thai chiles, stemmed, seeded, and minced
- 1  2"-piece ginger, peeled and minced
  Juice of 2 limes
- 1  cup coconut milk
- 2  tbsp. tamarind concentrate
- ½  tsp. curry powder
- ½  tsp. ground coriander
- ¼  tsp. cayenne pepper
  Canola oil, for brushing

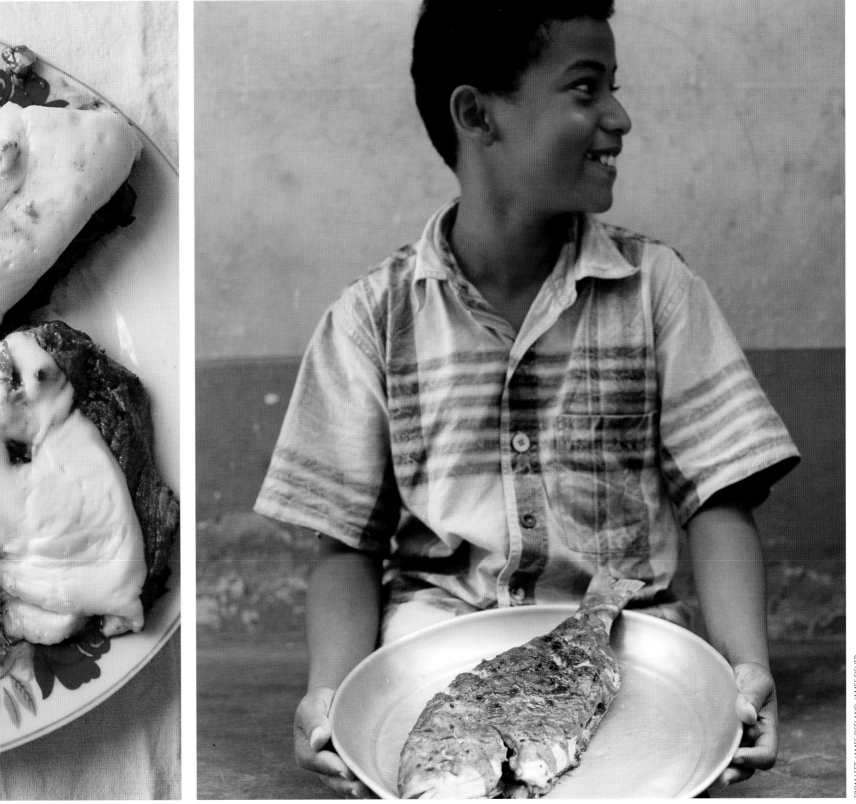

1 Put fish into a 9" x 13" baking dish and cut three evenly spaced ¼"-deep crosswise slits into each side of the fish. Season fish cavity and skin with salt and pepper. Combine garlic, chiles, ginger, and lime juice in a small bowl and rub cavity and skin of fish with the garlic mixture. Cover dish with plastic wrap and refrigerate for 1 hour. Meanwhile, heat the coconut milk, tamarind, curry powder, coriander, and cayenne in a 2-qt. saucepan over low heat and cook, stirring often, until tamarind is dissolved, about 2 minutes. Remove coconut sauce from the heat and set aside.

2 Build a medium-hot fire in a charcoal grill or heat a gas grill to medium-high. (Alternatively, arrange a rack 4" from broiler element and set oven to broil.) Brush fish with some of the coconut sauce. Grill fish, flipping every few minutes and basting often with the sauce, until cooked through, about 15 minutes. Transfer fish to a serving platter; serve hot or at room temperature.

## Pasta with Sardines
*(Pasta con le Sarde)*
SERVES 8
This saffron-tinged pasta dish has a sweet-savory tomato-based sauce bolstered with sardines, dried currants, and pine nuts. It's a standby among Sicilian home cooks like Giovanna Giglio Cascone (page 24).

1 cup olive oil
1½ lbs. cleaned fresh sardine filets
   Semolina flour, for dredging
2 medium fennel bulbs, finely chopped, fronds reserved
2 medium yellow onions, finely chopped
3 tbsp. tomato paste
6 oil-packed anchovy filets, drained and finely chopped
1 cup tomato sauce
3 tbsp. dried currants
3 tbsp. pine nuts
1 tsp. freshly grated nutmeg
¼ tsp. saffron
   Kosher salt and freshly ground black pepper, to taste
1 lb. spaghetti

1 Heat ¼ cup olive oil in a 10" skillet over medium-high heat. Toss 6 sardine filets in semolina to coat, shaking off excess, and then fry in oil until golden brown, about 4 minutes. Transfer to paper towels to drain, and then roughly chop and set aside to be used as a garnish.

2 Heat remaining oil in a 12" skillet over medium-high heat. Add fennel and onions, and cook, stirring occasionally, until caramelized, about 20 minutes. Roughly chop; add remaining sardines along with the tomato paste and anchovies, and cook, stirring often, until broken down and melted into the sauce, about 5 minutes. Add tomato sauce, currants, pine nuts, nutmeg, saffron, and salt and pepper; reduce heat to medium-low and cook, stirring occasionally, until thickened, about 20 minutes.

3 Bring a large pot of salted water to a boil and add pasta; cook until al dente, 7–8 minutes. Drain and transfer pasta to sauce along with fennel fronds and toss until evenly coated; top with reserved fried sardines, and serve immediately.

## Braised "Lion's Head" Meatballs with Napa Cabbage
*(Shi Zitou)*
SERVES 4
These ginger- and garlic-laced pork meatballs (pictured on page 240) are a specialty of home cook Eatty Du, a native of Shanghai, who makes them for her family in Las Vegas, Nevada (page 50).

1½ tsp. toasted sesame oil
10 leaves Napa cabbage
4 oz. enoki mushrooms, stems trimmed
¼ cup light soy sauce
1 tbsp. dark soy sauce
½ tsp. sugar
1 lb. ground pork
½ cup water chestnuts, minced
2 tsp. minced ginger
2 tsp. minced garlic
2 tbsp. cornstarch
2 tsp. Chinese cooking wine

1 Pour 1 tsp. sesame oil into a 6-qt. saucepan and arrange cabbage leaves on bottom in an even layer. Place mushrooms over the leaves in an even layer. Pour 2 tbsp. of the light soy sauce along with the dark soy sauce, sugar, and 1 cup water over mushrooms and leaves, and set aside.

2 In a bowl, combine pork, water chestnuts, ginger, and garlic. Add remaining sesame oil and soy sauce, along with cornstarch and wine; mix well. Divide mixture evenly into about eight 3-oz. meatballs; arrange meatballs in a single layer on top of cabbage. Bring to a simmer over medium-low heat; cook, covered, until cooked through, about 25 minutes.

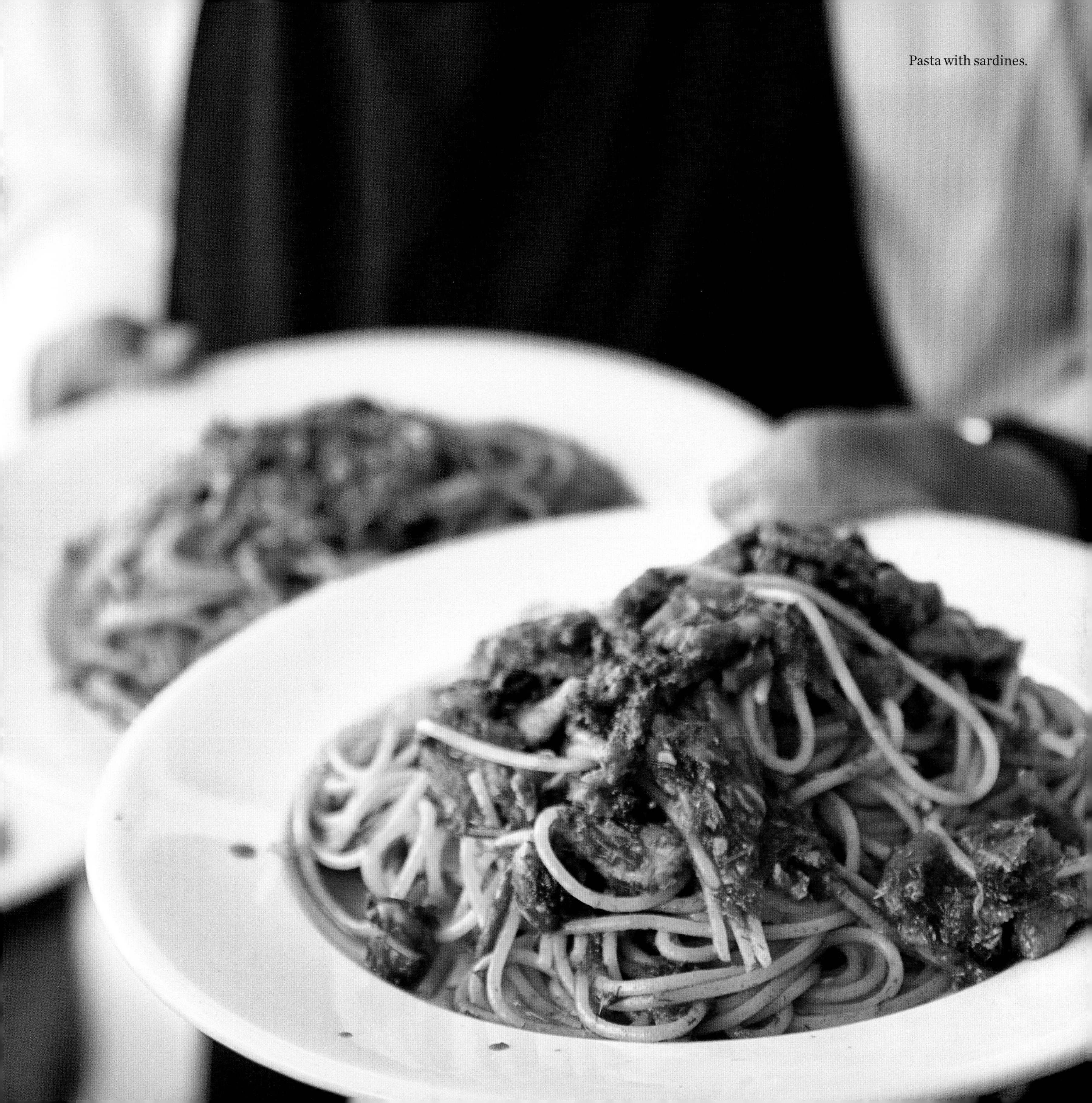

Pasta with sardines.

Braised "lion's head" meatballs with Napa cabbage (page 238).

# SIDE DISHES

Clockwise from top left: avocado-mango salad; stewed green beans; broccoli with Cheetos; pickled radishes and green onion.

## Avocado-Mango Salad

*(Saladu Awooka àk Mango)*

SERVES 4–6

In Dakar, Senegal (page 96), this salad, dressed with plenty of bright citrus juice, makes an ideal counterpoint to rich stews and meats.

- $1/2$ cup finely chopped parsley
- $1/4$ cup peanut or canola oil
- $1/4$ cup fresh lime juice
- 2 tbsp. fresh orange juice
- 1 jalapeño, stemmed, seeded, and minced
  Kosher salt and freshly ground black pepper, to taste
- 2 ripe mangoes, peeled, pitted, and cut into $1/4$" cubes
- 2 ripe avocados, pitted, peeled, and cut into 1" chunks
- 1 small navel orange, peeled and cut into segments
- 2 tsp. unsweetened shredded coconut (optional)

Whisk together 6 tbsp. parsley, the oil, both juices, jalapeño, and salt and pepper in a large bowl. Add mangoes and avocados, and toss gently to combine; cover with plastic wrap and refrigerate to meld flavors, about 1 hour. To serve, transfer avocado salad to a serving bowl; halve orange segments crosswise, and lay over salad. Sprinkle with remaining parsley and coconut, if you like. Serve chilled.

## Stewed Green Beans

SERVES 8–10

Infused with the meaty flavor of smoked turkey, these green beans are a favorite soul food side dish in restaurants like Martha Lou's Kitchen, in Charleston, South Carolina (page 15).

- 4 tbsp. unsalted butter, lard, or bacon fat
- 1 large yellow onion, roughly chopped
- 1 lb. green beans, strings removed
- 1 small smoked turkey leg
  Kosher salt and freshly ground black pepper, to taste

Heat butter in a 6-qt. saucepan over medium-high heat. Add onion and cook, stirring, until soft, about 4 minutes. Add green beans, turkey leg, and 4 cups water. Season with salt and pepper, and bring to a boil over high heat. Reduce heat to medium-low and cook, stirring, until green beans are very tender, about 1 hour. Remove turkey leg, shred meat off the bone, and stir meat back into the beans, if you like.

## Broccoli with Cheetos

SERVES 6

Chef Craig Koketsu of New York's Park Avenue restaurant (page 150) uses crunchy Cheetos as a textural foil for broccoli served with a creamy Gouda-and-Parmesan sauce.

- 2 cups heavy cream
- 3 tbsp. minced garlic
- 2 tbsp. minced shallots
- 6 black peppercorns
- 1 bay leaf
- $1 1/2$ cups grated aged Gouda
- $1/2$ cup grated Parmesan
  Kosher salt, to taste
- $1 1/4$ lbs. (about 2 large heads) broccoli, cut into small florets, stems cut crosswise into $1/4$" slices
- 3 tbsp. extra-virgin olive oil
- 1 tsp. crushed red chile flakes
- 2 cups original Cheetos, crushed by hand

1 Make the cheese sauce: Heat cream, 2 tbsp. garlic, shallots, peppercorns, and bay leaf in a 2-qt. saucepan over medium-high heat. Cook, stirring often, until reduced by half, about 6 minutes. Remove pan from heat, stir in cheeses until melted, and season with salt. Set a fine strainer over a small saucepan and strain sauce, discarding solids. Keep sauce warm over low heat until ready to serve.

2 Bring a large pot of salted water to a boil over high heat. Add broccoli and cook, stirring, until crisp-tender, about 3 minutes. Drain broccoli, transfer to a bowl of ice water, and let chill. Drain and transfer to paper towels to dry; set aside. Heat oil in a 12" skillet over medium-high heat. Add remaining garlic and chile flakes and cook until fragrant, 1 minute. Add broccoli and cook, stirring often, until just subtly browned, about 6 minutes. To serve, spoon cheese sauce evenly among 6 warm serving bowls or small plates. Top sauce with broccoli and a generous sprinkling of Cheetos. Serve immediately.

## Pickled Radishes and Green Onion

SERVES 4

Crisp, lightly pickled radishes, frequently served at the Las Vegas table of home cook Eatty Du (page 50), get their balanced, savory-sweet flavor from a quick cure in sesame oil and sugar.

- 2 cups Japanese baby radishes, quartered or halved (depending on size)
- 1 tsp. kosher salt
- 1 tsp. sugar
- 2 tsp. toasted sesame oil
- 1 scallion, thinly sliced

Toss radishes, salt, and sugar together in a bowl, then chill in refrigerator for at least 1 hour. Drain excess liquid, and mix with sesame oil and scallion. Serve immediately.

## Buttermilk Biscuits

MAKES 15 LARGE BISCUITS

The secret to these ultra-fluffy biscuits, made at the First Baptist Church in Kosciusko, Mississippi (page 119), is to work the dough as little as possible.

7 1/2 cups flour
3 tbsp. baking powder
1 tbsp. sugar
1 3/4 tsp. kosher salt
1 tsp. baking soda
3/4 lb. unsalted butter, chilled and cut into small cubes
2 cups buttermilk
1 cup half-and-half

**1** Heat oven to 375°. Whisk together the flour, baking powder, sugar, salt, and baking soda in a large bowl. Add butter to the flour mixture; use your fingers to break apart butter pieces, while working them into the flour mixture, until pea-size pieces form. In a small bowl, whisk together the buttermilk and half-and-half. Pour the buttermilk mixture over the flour mixture and, using a rubber spatula, mix the ingredients until just combined.

**2** Turn the dough out onto a well-floured surface. Pat the dough into a single mass, and gently press it into a 1"-thick disk. Gently roll the dough once with a rolling pin to create a smooth surface. Using a 2 3/4" round cookie cutter, cut out biscuits and transfer them to a parchment paper–lined baking pan. Arrange the biscuits in the center of the pan so that their edges touch (this will help to keep them moist). Reroll the scraps, and cut out more biscuits until all the dough is used. Bake until golden brown, 30–35 minutes. Transfer the baking sheet to a rack; let cool for 5 minutes before serving.

## Dry-Cured Olives with Rosemary and Orange

SERVES 6–8

This simple recipe for dry-cured black olives flavored with orange zest and fresh rosemary exemplifies the full-bodied flavors of the Sicilian kitchen. Home cooks like Giovanna Giglio Cascone (page 24) put them out to pique the appetite.

1 orange
1 lb. dry-cured black olives
1 large sprig rosemary, stemmed and roughly chopped
Freshly ground black pepper, to taste

**1** Wash orange thoroughly; dry. Using a vegetable peeler, remove zest from orange, taking care to peel as little of the white pith as possible; roughly chop zest and transfer to a medium bowl.

**2** Juice orange and add juice to zest along with olives, rosemary, and pepper; toss to coat. Let sit at room temperature for 1 hour to marinate before serving.

## Cheese and Bread Soup
*(Soupe Crasse)*

SERVES 8–10

Like many home cooks in the Italian Alps, Lucia Gros Corradin (page 194) makes this substantial soup—more like a rich casserole of melted cheese and bread—during the Christmas holidays each year.

3 1/2 cups beef or chicken stock
5 tbsp. unsalted butter
10 oz. Italian breadsticks
1 lb. Taleggio cheese, sliced
Kosher salt and freshly ground black pepper, to taste
1/2 small onion, thinly sliced

**1** Bring stock to a boil in a 1-qt. saucepan; remove from heat. Grease bottom of a 3-qt. high-sided skillet with 1 tbsp. butter. Break breadsticks into 2 1/2" pieces. Put 1 layer breadsticks in skillet. Cover breadsticks with a layer of cheese. Continue layering breadsticks and cheese; ladle stock over breadsticks one ladleful at a time and heat skillet over low heat. Bring to a simmer; cook, without stirring, for 30 minutes.

**2** Meanwhile, melt remaining butter in a 12" skillet over medium heat. Add onion; cook, until onion is soft, 8–10 minutes. Set a fine sieve over a small bowl. Strain butter, pressing onion with back of a spoon; discard onion. Drizzle butter over soup; continue cooking for 10 more minutes. To serve, spoon onto serving plates.

## Fennel and Herb Phyllo Pastries
*(Hortopita)*

MAKES 10–12 PASTRIES

Los Angeles home cook Marino Pascal (page 2) shared his family's recipe for these flaky pies filled with fragrant fennel and briny feta cheese.

4 tbsp. extra-virgin olive oil
1 bunch Swiss chard (about 1 3/4 lbs.), stemmed and chopped
1/2 small white onion, minced
1/2 small bulb fennel (with stalks and fronds), minced
3 oz. feta, crumbled
1 tbsp. minced flat-leaf parsley
3 scallions, thinly sliced
Kosher salt and freshly ground black pepper, to taste
1 (16-oz.) package frozen phyllo dough, thawed
6 tbsp. unsalted butter, melted

**1** Heat 2 tbsp. oil in a 12" nonstick skillet over high heat. Working in 2 batches, add chard and cook, stirring frequently, until wilted, about 4 minutes. Transfer chard to a large sieve and press with a wooden spoon to extract excess liquid; set aside. Return skillet to medium-high heat and add remaining oil. Add onion and fennel, and cook, stirring occasionally, until soft, about 20 minutes. Transfer onion mixture to a bowl; stir in chard, feta, parsley, and scallions. Season filling with salt and pepper; let chill.

**2** Heat oven to 375°. Cut stacked sheets of phyllo lengthwise into 4 1/2"-wide strips; cover with a damp towel. Set aside. Put 1 strip phyllo on a surface and brush with some of the butter; top with another strip and brush with more butter. Repeat once more. Put ⅓ cup filling on one end of strip 1" from the end. Fold in a corner of that end to form a triangle. Then fold in that triangular edge to form another triangle; continue folding as you would a flag, until you have a triangular pastry. Transfer pastry to a baking sheet. Repeat; brush pastries with remaining butter. Bake until golden brown, 18–20 minutes.

## Umbrian Vegetable Soup
*(Zuppa di Verdure all'Agliata)*
SERVES 12
A family recipe of the Italian chef Lidia Bastianich (page 214), this soup is cooked quickly to preserve the vegetables' fresh flavors.

- ½ cup packed basil leaves
- ¼ cup extra-virgin olive oil, plus more for drizzling
- 2 tbsp. minced flat-leaf parsley
- 4 cloves garlic
- ½ medium yellow onion, roughly chopped
- 8 oz. red new potatoes, cut into ½" cubes
- 3 ribs celery, minced
- 2 medium carrots, minced
- 2 plum tomatoes, cored and minced
  Kosher salt, to taste
- 3 oz. spinach, trimmed and rinsed (about 2 loosely packed cups)
- 1½ cups canned cannellini beans, rinsed
- 1 cup fresh or frozen green peas
- ½ small head frisée, leaves cut into bite-size pieces (about 2 cups)
  Freshly ground black pepper, to taste
  Freshly grated Parmesan, for serving

1 Place half the basil, 2 tbsp. oil, parsley, garlic, and onion in the bowl of a food processor, and process until slightly chunky; set paste aside.

2 Heat remaining oil in an 8-qt. pot over medium-high heat, and add herb–garlic paste; cook, stirring often, until no liquid remains, about 5 minutes. Add potatoes, celery, carrots, and tomatoes. Cook, stirring often, until vegetables are golden brown, about 6 minutes. Add salt and 4 cups water, and bring to a boil. Reduce heat to medium-low; cover and cook, stirring occasionally, until vegetables are tender, about 20 minutes.

3 Stir in spinach, beans, peas, and frisée, and cook until greens are wilted and just tender, about 10 minutes; season with salt and pepper, and stir in remaining basil. To serve, ladle soup into bowls, sprinkle with Parmesan, and drizzle with oil.

## Indian Flatbread
*(Chapati)*
MAKES 10 FLATBREADS
Thinner and chewier than *paratha* or *naan,* these nutty Indian flatbreads (pictured on page 108) are made with whole durum wheat flour, which lends an earthy depth.

- 2 cups Indian durum wheat flour (also known as *atta*)
- 1 tbsp. kosher salt
- 1 tbsp. clarified butter or canola oil, plus more for brushing

1 Stir together flour, salt, butter, and 1 cup water in a bowl until dough forms. Transfer to a work surface, and knead until smooth, about 4 minutes. Cover with plastic wrap, and let sit for 1 hour. Divide dough into 10 equal pieces, and shape each piece into a ball. Using a rolling pin, roll each ball into a 5" round.

2 Heat a 12" cast-iron skillet over high heat. Add 1 dough round and cook, turning once, until cooked through and charred in spots, about 2 minutes. Transfer to a plate, and brush on both sides with butter; repeat with remaining rounds. Serve hot.

## New Orleans Oyster Stew
SERVES 6
Rich and creamy oyster stew is a restaurant classic and a popular first course during the holidays in New Orleans.

- 50 medium oysters, such as blue points, shucked (about 1½ lbs.), with 1 cup of the liquor reserved
- 12 tbsp. unsalted butter
- 5 tbsp. flour
- 4 ribs celery, finely chopped
- 4 cloves garlic, finely chopped
- 1 large onion, finely chopped
- ½ cup finely chopped parsley
- 1 tbsp. kosher salt
- 1½ tsp. ground black pepper
- ¼ tsp. cayenne
- 2 cups milk
- 2 cups heavy cream

1 Combine oyster liquor with 1 cup water in a 2-qt. saucepan. Bring to a simmer over medium heat. Add the oysters, and simmer until their edges just begin to curl, about 2 minutes. Strain oysters through a fine strainer set over a medium bowl. Reserve oysters and cooking liquid separately.

2 Heat butter in a 4-qt. saucepan over medium-high heat. Add flour and cook, whisking constantly, until golden brown, 3–4 minutes. Reduce heat to medium; add celery, garlic, onion, parsley, salt, pepper, and cayenne. Cook, stirring frequently with a wooden spoon, until onions and celery are very soft, about 25 minutes. Stir in milk, cream, and reserved oysters with their cooking liquid and cook, stirring occasionally, until just hot, about 5 minutes. Serve immediately.

From left: chickpeas with pickled mango; stewed rutabagas.

## Chickpeas with Pickled Mango

SERVES 6

The food trucks of Portland, Oregon (page 164) are full of culinary surprises—for instance, these slow-cooked chickpeas with tomato, mango, and sumac, from Nawal Sahbi of Aladdin's Castle Café.

- 1 lb. dried chickpeas, soaked overnight
- 1/2 cup roughly chopped pickled mango
- 1 tbsp. sumac
- 1 medium tomato, cored and roughly chopped
  Kosher salt and freshly ground black pepper, to taste

1 Drain beans and place in a 4-qt. saucepan, cover with water by 2", and bring to a boil over high heat; reduce heat to medium-low, and cook, covered and stirring occasionally, until tender, about 25 minutes.

2 Drain beans, and transfer to a bowl; add pickled mango, sumac, tomato, and salt and pepper; let sit for 30 minutes to meld flavors before serving with flatbread.

## Stewed Rutabagas

SERVES 8–10

In Charleston soul food restaurants (page 15), this inventive take on rutabagas involves stewing them with pork neck bones and ginger, then caramelizing them with sugar to deepen the flavor.

- 1/4 cup canola oil
- 1 tsp. dried thyme
- 4 cloves garlic, finely chopped
- 2 ribs celery, finely chopped
- 1 large yellow onion, finely chopped
- 1 1"–piece ginger, peeled and finely grated
  Kosher salt and freshly ground black pepper, to taste
- 3 lb. rutabagas, peeled, cut into 3/4" cubes
- 8 oz. smoked pork neck bones
- 4 tsp. sugar
- 1 1/2 cups chicken stock

Heat oven to 400°. Heat oil in a 12" skillet over medium-high heat. Add thyme, garlic, celery, onion, ginger, salt and pepper, and cook, stirring, until soft, about 4 minutes. Transfer to a 9" x 13" baking dish, and stir in rutabagas and pork bones; sprinkle with 2 tsp. sugar, and add stock. Cover with aluminum foil; bake until rutabagas are tender, about 1 hour. Uncover, and remove pork bones; cut meat away from bones, roughly chop, and return to rutabagas. Sprinkle rutabagas with remaining sugar, stir to combine, and continue baking until caramelized, about 5 minutes.

Layered herring salad (page 250).

248

## Layered Herring Salad
*(Selyodka Pod Shuboy)*
SERVES 6–8

Latvian home cook Stanislava Balsa (page 154) blankets salt-cured herring in apples, boiled root vegetables, and a sour cream–mayonnaise dressing to make this lavish and visually striking salad (pictured on page 248).

1 cup mayonnaise
1 cup sour cream
 Kosher salt and freshly ground black pepper, to taste
3 filets salted herring, rinsed and roughly chopped
½ small yellow onion, minced
2 medium peeled and boiled Yukon Gold potatoes, grated
3 medium boiled carrots, grated
6 hard-boiled eggs, whites and yolks separated, each passed through a fine strainer
½ Granny Smith apple, cored, peeled, and grated
2 medium boiled beets, peeled and grated
¼ cup chopped fresh dill
 Carrot rose, for garnish (optional)

Whisk together mayonnaise and sour cream in a small bowl and season with salt and pepper; set aside. Place herring in the bottom of a shallow 1½-qt. oval dish, and top with ⅓ dressing. Sprinkle onion on top, then cover with grated potatoes. Top potatoes with carrots and half the remaining dressing. Combine half the sieved egg yolks and half the sieved whites in a small bowl, then spread over dressing. Top with apples, then beets. Spread remaining dressing over beets to cover. Create three even rows across top of salad with remaining egg yolks and three rows with remaining whites; fill in gaps with rows of dill. Garnish with a carrot rose, if you like.

## Bistro French Fries
*(Bistro Pommes Frites)*
SERVES 4

The secret to stellar bistro fries (pictured on page 9) is duck fat, a superior frying medium that gives the potatoes a deep, meaty flavor.

7 cups duck fat
3 cups canola oil
4 large russet potatoes, cut lengthwise into ¼"-thick batons
 Kosher salt, to taste

1 Heat duck fat and oil in a 6-qt. Dutch oven over medium-high heat until a deep-fry thermometer reads 325°. Working in small batches, add potatoes and cook, turning occasionally and maintaining a temperature of 300° (the temperature will drop when you add the potatoes), until pale and tender, 5–6 minutes. Using a slotted spoon, transfer fries to a wire rack set over a baking sheet. Remove pot from heat, and refrigerate fries for 1 hour.

2 Return oil to medium-high heat until a deep-fry thermometer reads 400°. Working in small batches, add chilled fries to oil and cook, turning occasionally and maintaining a temperature of 375°, until golden brown and crisp, 1–2 minutes. Using a slotted spoon, transfer fries to a rack set over a baking sheet; season with salt. Serve hot.

## Ricotta Crostini with Black Olives, Lemon Zest, and Mint
SERVES 4–6

In Torre Melissa, Italy (page 69), peasant bread heaped with ricotta cheese gets a boost of bold flavor with the addition of lemon zest, pungent cured olives, and refreshing mint (pictured on page 256).

1 loaf of ciabatta or another peasant-style bread
 Extra-virgin olive oil, for drizzling
1 clove garlic, peeled
1½ cups ricotta cheese, at room temperature
 Oil-cured black olives, pitted and chopped
 Lemon zest
 Mint leaves, torn into pieces

Prepare a medium-hot charcoal fire in a grill or set gas grill to medium-high heat. Cut bread into ½"-thick crosswise slices. Drizzle the bread with olive oil. Grill bread slices until both sides have grill marks and slightly charred crusts, 4–5 minutes. While hot, rub bread with garlic. Slather 1 tbsp. of the ricotta on top of each toasted slice. Spread olives, lemon zest, and torn mint atop ricotta.

## Ricotta Crostini with Cherry Tomatoes
SERVES 4–6

Ricotta and cherry tomatoes, sautéed until bursting, are spooned over toast to make an appetizer or a light meal (pictured on page 256).

1 cup cherry tomatoes
 Extra-virgin olive oil, for drizzling
 Kosher salt and freshly ground black pepper, to taste
1 loaf of ciabatta or another peasant-style bread
1 clove garlic, peeled
1½ cups ricotta cheese, at room temperature
 Parmesan cheese

1 Place tomatoes in a 10" skillet over medium-high heat, drizzle with olive oil, season with salt and pepper; cook until the tomatoes have burst and started to release their juices, about 8 minutes. Set aside.

2 Prepare a medium-hot charcoal fire in a grill or set gas grill to medium-high heat. Cut bread into ½"-thick crosswise slices. Drizzle the bread with olive oil. Grill bread slices until both sides have grill marks and slightly charred crusts, 4–5 minutes. While hot, rub bread

with garlic. Slather 1 tbsp. of the ricotta on top of each toasted slice. Spoon cherry tomatoes onto ricotta. Garnish with thin shavings of Parmesan cheese and more black pepper.

## Ricotta Crostini with Chestnut Honey

SERVES 4-6

Crusty bread topped with silky ricotta and sweet honey is a perfect snack, morning, noon, or night (pictured on page 256).

- 1 loaf of ciabatta or another peasant-style bread Extra-virgin olive oil, for drizzling
- 1½ cups ricotta cheese, at room temperature Chestnut honey

Prepare a medium-hot charcoal fire in a grill or set gas grill to medium-high heat. Cut bread into ½"-thick crosswise slices. Drizzle the bread with olive oil. Grill bread slices until both sides have grill marks and slightly charred crusts, 4–5 minutes. Slather a heaping dollop of room-temperature ricotta on top of each toasted slice. Top ricotta with a drizzle of chestnut honey.

## Ricotta Crostini with Soppressata

SERVES 4-6

Creamy cow's or sheep's milk ricotta pairs beautifully with soppressata salami atop these rustic crostini (pictured on page 256).

- 1 loaf of ciabatta or another peasant-style bread Extra-virgin olive oil, for drizzling
- 1 clove garlic, peeled
- 1½ cups ricotta cheese, at room temperature
- 24 thin coins of soppressata

Prepare a medium-hot charcoal fire in a grill or set gas grill to medium-high. Cut bread into ½"-thick crosswise slices. Drizzle the bread with olive oil. Grill bread slices until both sides have grill marks and slightly charred crusts, 4–5 minutes. While hot, rub bread with garlic. Slather 1 tbsp. of the ricotta on top of each toasted slice. Top ricotta with 3–4 thin coins of soppressata.

## Cape Breton Potato Salad

SERVES 6-8

Stirring in the radishes, scallions, and celery at the last minute, after the potatoes have cooled, preserves their crisp bite. The recipe for this salad (pictured on page 257) comes from Charlene Murphy of Cape Breton Island, Canada (page 129).

- 8 red and white small new potatoes (about 1½ lbs.), cut crosswise into ¼"-thick rounds Kosher salt, to taste
- ¼ cup extra-virgin olive oil
- ¼ cup red wine vinegar
- 1 tbsp. Dijon mustard
- 2 cloves garlic, finely chopped Freshly ground black pepper, to taste
- ¼ cup flat-leaf parsley leaves, roughly chopped
- 5 small red radishes, trimmed and thinly sliced crosswise
- 5 scallions, thinly sliced crosswise
- 2 ribs celery, finely chopped

1 Put potatoes into a 6-qt. saucepan with enough salted water to cover the potatoes by 1". Cover the pan, and bring water to a boil over high heat. Uncover, reduce heat to medium-low, and simmer until potatoes are tender, about 10 minutes. Drain potatoes, and transfer to a large bowl.

2 In a small bowl, whisk together the oil, vinegar, mustard, garlic, and salt and pepper; pour vinaigrette over the potatoes and toss gently to combine. Let cool for 10 minutes; stir in the parsley, radishes, scallions, and celery just before serving.

From left: yogurt and cucumber; Gujurati cabbage.

## Yogurt and Cucumber

*(Mast-o Khiar)*

MAKES 2 CUPS

Sweetened with golden raisins and perfumed with rose petals, this creamy dip is served with flatbread or alongside rice or lamb, on the tables of Iranian families like the Abbas Nejads (page 160), who live in Iran's north.

10 tbsp. golden raisins
1 clove garlic, minced
   Kosher salt, to taste
1 lb. plus 2 oz. plain yogurt
1 tbsp. dried mint
3 medium cucumbers, peeled
   Dried rose petals, for garnish

Soak raisins in warm water until soft, 8–10 minutes; drain. Place garlic on a cutting board and sprinkle with kosher salt; using a knife, mash into a paste. Transfer to bowl along with 8 tbsp. raisins, yogurt, and mint; seed and mince cucumbers, and stir into yogurt mixture. Garnish with remaining raisins and rose petals. Let chill before serving.

## Gujarati Cabbage

*(Kobi Nu Shaak)*

SERVES 4–6

To achieve the right texture for this fragrant Indian side dish, it's crucial to salt the cabbage before cooking in order to extract some of its moisture. This recipe comes from home cook Varshaben Chauhan (page 110), who lives in the city of Ahmedabad.

1 green cabbage, cored
   and shredded
   Kosher salt, to taste
2 tbsp. peanut oil
2 tsp. black mustard seeds
2 tsp. asafetida
2 tsp. cumin seeds
10 fresh curry leaves
2 tsp. ground turmeric
3 plum tomatoes, chopped
3 Italian frying peppers, seeded and thinly sliced crosswise
1 serrano chile, thinly sliced
5 tbsp. roughly chopped cilantro
¼ cup fresh lime juice
2 tbsp. sugar

Toss cabbage and salt in a bowl. Let wilt for 1 hour. Squeeze excess liquid from cabbage; set aside. Heat oil in a 12" skillet over medium-high heat. Add mustard seeds, asafetida, cumin, and curry leaves; cook, stirring, until fragrant, about 2 minutes. Add reserved cabbage, turmeric, tomatoes, peppers, and chile; cook, stirring, until cabbage is crisp-tender, 6–7 minutes. Stir in cilantro, lime juice, and sugar. Season with salt; cook until flavors meld, 3–5 minutes.

Clockwise from top left: rice and beans; black-eyed pea salad; feta tart; fish croquettes in spiced tomato sauce (page 235).

## Rice and Beans
*(Baião-de-Dois)*

SERVES 8–10

Rice and beans is a staple side dish across Latin America. On the island of Marajó, in northern Brazil (page 170), bacon and chorizo are rendered down with annatto to make a meaty and deeply savory version.

2 tbsp. olive oil
8 oz. bacon, cut into $1/4$" cubes
5 oz. dried chorizo, cut into $1/4$" cubes
1 medium yellow onion, finely chopped
6 cloves garlic, finely chopped
2 tsp. ground annatto (optional)
1 lb. dried black-eyed peas, soaked overnight, drained
$2 1/2$ cups jasmine rice, rinsed in a strainer until water runs clear, drained
Kosher salt and freshly ground black pepper, to taste

Heat oil in an 8-qt saucepan over medium-high heat. Add bacon, and cook, stirring, until fat is rendered, about 12 minutes. Add chorizo, and cook until fat begins to render, about 5 minutes. Add onion and cook, stirring, until soft, about 6 minutes. Add garlic, and cook, stirring, until golden brown, about 9 minutes. Add annatto, and cook until fragrant, about 1 minute. Add peas and $5 1/2$ cups water, and bring to a boil. Cover partially with a lid, and reduce heat to medium; cook until peas are tender, about 30 minutes. Add rice,

and bring to a boil; cover pot, reduce heat to low, and cook until rice is tender, about 20 minutes. Remove from the heat and season with salt and pepper before serving.

## Black-Eyed Pea Salad
*(Saladu Ñebbe)*

SERVES 8

This Senegalese salad of black-eyed peas and vegetables spiced with chiles is great as a side dish or a lunch on its own.

$1 3/4$ lb. cooked black-eyed peas
1 cup canola oil
1 cup roughly chopped parsley
$1/4$ cup fresh lime juice
10 scallions, roughly chopped
1 red bell pepper, stemmed, seeded, and finely chopped
1 medium tomato, cored, seeded, and finely chopped
1 medium cucumber, seeded and finely chopped
1 habañero or Scotch bonnet chile, stemmed, seeded, and minced
Kosher salt and freshly ground black pepper, to taste

Place all ingredients in a large bowl, and stir to combine; refrigerate at least 1 hour to marinate and meld flavors. Serve chilled or at room temperature.

## Feta Tart
*(Alevropita)*

SERVES 8–10

Made with a simple egg batter and layered with crumbled feta cheese, this soul-satisfying tart is a specialty of the Epirus region of northern Greece (page 36).

6 tbsp. extra-virgin olive oil
2 tsp. vodka
1 egg
$1 1/4$ cups flour, sifted
$1/4$ tsp. kosher salt
$1/8$ tsp. baking powder
10 oz. feta, crumbled
2 tbsp. unsalted butter, softened

**1** Heat oven to 500°. Put an 18" x 13" x 1" rimmed baking sheet into oven for 10 minutes. Meanwhile, whisk together 2 tbsp. oil, vodka, egg, and 1 cup water in a bowl. In a separate bowl, whisk together flour, salt, and baking powder. Pour wet mixture over dry mixture, and whisk together until smooth.

**2** Brush remaining oil over bottom of hot pan, and add batter, smoothing with a rubber spatula to coat the bottom evenly. Distribute cheese evenly over batter, and dot with butter. Bake, rotating baking sheet halfway through, until golden brown and crunchy, about 20 minutes. Let cool slightly before slicing and serving.

Facing page, clockwise from top left: ricotta crostini topped with cherry tomatoes; black olives, lemon zest, and mint; chestnut honey; and soppressata (pages 250–251). Above, Cape Breton potato salad (page 251).

ANDRÉ BARANOWSKI (2)

257

# DESSERTS

## Ricotta and Coffee Mousse
*(Spuma di Ricotta al Caffè)*
SERVES 6

Rich ricotta is the star of this elegant and easy Calabrian dessert, made light and smooth with the additions of whipped cream and gelatin. Espresso and grated bittersweet chocolate lend intense flavors to the mousse.

- 2 cups store-bought or homemade ricotta
- 1 cup cold heavy cream
- 1/3 cup sugar
- 1 tbsp. unflavored powdered gelatin
- 2 tbsp. instant espresso
  Shaved bittersweet chocolate, for garnish

1 Purée ricotta in a blender until smooth. Transfer to a large bowl; set aside.

2 Whip together heavy cream and sugar in a large bowl until soft peaks form; set aside.

3 Sprinkle gelatin over 2 tbsp. cold water in a small bowl and let sit until softened, about 5 minutes. Add espresso and 2 tbsp. boiling water, and stir until espresso and gelatin dissolve.

4 Stir espresso and gelatin mixture into ricotta; fold in cream in 3 stages. Chill mixture for 1 hour, then transfer to a pastry bag fitted with a star tip. Pipe mixture into 6 serving glasses; refrigerate until set, about 1 hour. Garnish with shaved chocolate.

## Waffle Cones Filled with Sweet Cheese and Berries
*(Pildītas Vafeles)*
MAKES ABOUT 20 CONES

Latvian home cook Maija Kalnina (page 86) shared the recipe for this summertime dessert of crisp homemade waffle cones filled with sweetened cheese and tart raspberries (pictured on page 260).

- 1 1/2 cups sugar
- 14 tbsp. unsalted butter, softened
- 2 tsp. vanilla extract
- 5 eggs
- 1 cup flour
- 1 tsp. cornstarch
- 8 oz. farmer's cheese or cottage cheese, drained overnight in a cheesecloth-lined strainer
- 1 3/4 cups heavy cream
- 1 cup raspberries

1 Make the waffles: Beat together 1 cup sugar, butter, and 1 tsp. vanilla on medium speed of a handheld mixer until pale and fluffy, about 2 minutes. Add eggs, one at a time, until smooth. Add flour and cornstarch, and mix until just combined; let batter sit for 10 minutes.

2 Heat a small, thin waffle iron or krumkake maker. Working in batches, add 2 tbsp. batter to each mold, and cook until waffles are lightly browned, about 45 seconds. Quickly form waffles into wide, shallow cones; let harden.

3 Make the filling: Combine remaining sugar and cheese in a food processor; process until smooth. Beat remaining vanilla and cream in a large bowl until stiff peaks form; add cheese mixture to whipped cream, and gently fold to combine. Chill.

4 To serve, transfer cheese mixture to a piping bag fitted with a plain tip and pipe about 2 tbsp. mixture into each cone. Add some berries, and continue layering cheese mixture and berries to fill. Serve immediately.

## Brazilian Banana Pudding
*(Sombremesa de Banana com Queijo)*
SERVES 6–8

This confection of fresh bananas layered with cream cheese and homemade *dulce de leche,* a specialty of Marajó Island in northern Brazil (page 170), has a touch of warm cinnamon spice.

- 1 14-oz. can sweetened condensed milk
- 1 12-oz. can evaporated milk
- 1 stick cinnamon
- 1 tbsp. unsalted butter, for greasing
- 4 very ripe bananas, cut crosswise into 2" lengths and then lengthwise into 1/4"-thick slices
- 12 oz. cream cheese, cut into 1/2" cubes, softened
- 1/4 tsp. ground cinnamon

1 Heat oven to 350°. Bring both milks and cinnamon stick to a boil in 12" nonstick skillet over medium-high heat; reduce heat to medium, and cook, stirring occasionally, until reduced by half, light brown in color, and very thick, about 30 minutes. Discard cinnamon stick, and set reduced milk aside.

2 Grease an 8"x 8" glass baking dish with butter. Spread 1/3 of the reduced milk over bottom of dish; top with half the bananas, and then dot with half the cream cheese. Pour over half of remaining reduced milk, top with remaining bananas, and dot with remaining cheese; pour over remaining reduced milk.

3 Sprinkle ground cinnamon over top, and bake until cheese is melted and bubbly, about 30 minutes. Let cool for 10 minutes before serving.

## Apricot Cake
*(Prăjitură Cu Caise)*
SERVES 12

This simple sour-cream cake (pictured on page 260), scented with lemon zest and dotted with ripe apricot halves, is typical of the rustic cuisine of rural Transylvania, in north central Romania (page 183).

Unsalted butter, for pan
2 ³/₄ cups flour, plus more for pan
1 tsp. baking powder
¹/₂ tsp. kosher salt
1 ¹/₂ cups sugar, plus 1 tbsp. for sprinkling
1 tsp. lemon zest
4 eggs
³/₄ cup canola oil
³/₄ cup sour cream
¹/₂ cup milk
1 tsp. vanilla extract
6 apricots (about 1 ¹/₂ lb.), halved and pitted

1 Heat oven to 350°. Grease and flour a 9" x 13" baking pan; set aside. Whisk together flour, baking powder, and salt in a bowl; set aside.

2 In a large bowl, beat 1 ¹/₂ cups sugar, zest, and eggs on medium-high speed of a mixer until pale and tripled in volume, about 5 minutes. Add oil, sour cream, milk, and vanilla, and beat until smooth. Add dry ingredients, and stir just until combined. Pour batter into prepared pan, and smooth top with a rubber spatula; place apricot halves, cut sides up, evenly over batter.

3 Sprinkle top of cake and apricots with remaining sugar, and bake until a toothpick inserted into middle

of cake comes out clean, about 45 minutes. Let cool, and cut into squares to serve.

## Pineapple Upside-Down Cake

SERVES 8
This recipe comes from the chief of the Arcata Fire Department in Humboldt County, California (page 56). The butter, brown sugar, and brandy cooked in the bottom of the skillet make a sumptuous caramelized topping.

1 ³/₄ cups flour
2 tsp. baking powder
¹/₄ tsp. kosher salt
1 ¹/₃ cups unsalted butter
1 cup sugar
1 tbsp. distilled white vinegar
3 tsp. vanilla
3 eggs
¹/₃ cup low-fat buttermilk
10 tbsp. dark brown sugar
2 tbsp. brandy
7 slices canned pineapple
¹/₂ cup stemmed maraschino cherries

1 Heat oven to 350°. In a bowl, whisk together flour, baking powder, and salt; set aside. In a large bowl, beat together 12 tbsp. butter, sugar, vinegar, and 2 tsp. vanilla on medium-high speed of a handheld mixer until fluffy, about 4 minutes. Add eggs, one at a time, to butter mixture, beating for 15 seconds between each addition. Working in three batches, alternately

add flour mixture and buttermilk to batter, beating on low speed until just combined. Scrape down sides of the bowl. Beat batter on medium speed until smooth, about 3 minutes. Set aside.

1 Melt remaining butter in a 10" nonstick skillet over medium-high heat. Whisk in remaining vanilla, brown sugar, and brandy until dissolved, 1 minute. Remove skillet from heat; arrange pineapple slices across bottom of skillet. Arrange cherries evenly among the slices. Pour in cake batter. Bake until cake is golden and set, about 35 minutes.

2 Let cake cool for 30 minutes before unmolding onto a large serving platter. This allows the caramel to set into the fruit and cake without hardening and sticking to the pan.

## Amadeus Cookies

MAKES 24 COOKIES
These chocolate-dipped sandwich cookies filled with a combination of pistachios and almond paste (pictured on page 261) are a specialty of the pastry shop Demel in Vienna, Austria (page 70).

FOR THE COOKIES:
1 ³/₄ cups flour
12 tbsp. unsalted butter, softened
³/₄ cup confectioners' sugar
2 egg yolks
¹/₂ tsp. kosher salt

FOR THE FILLING:
¹/₂ cup shelled and unsalted pistachios
1 tbsp. sugar
3 ¹/₂ oz. almond paste, at room temperature, chopped
2 tbsp. cherry liqueur, such as kirsch
¹/₂ tsp. vanilla extract

FOR THE GLAZE:
¹/₂ cup sugar
3 tbsp. light corn syrup
4 oz. semisweet chocolate, preferably 54%, roughly chopped

1 Make the cookie dough: In a bowl, beat ¹/₂ cup flour, the butter, and confectioners' sugar with a handheld mixer on medium speed until pale and fluffy, 1–2 minutes. Add yolks one at a time, beating until smooth after each addition. Add salt and remaining flour; beat to make dough. Halve dough, flatten into 2 disks, and wrap each with plastic wrap. Refrigerate dough for 1 hour.

2 Make the filling: In the bowl of a food processor, process the pistachios with the sugar until finely ground. Add almond paste, and process until combined. Add the kirsch and vanilla, and process until smooth; set filling aside.

3 Heat oven to 325°. Transfer 1 dough disk to a lightly floured

From left: waffle cone filled with sweet cheese and berries (page 258); apricot cake (page 258); Amadeus cookies (page 259).

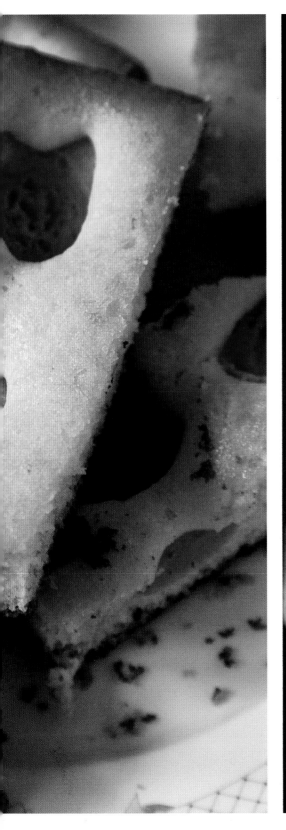

Strawberry cake.

surface and roll with a floured rolling pin to a ⅛" thickness. Using a 1¾" round cookie cutter, cut out 24 cookies. Repeat with remaining dough disk. (Combine and reroll scraps to make 48 cookies in all.) Place cookies 1" apart on 2 parchment paper–lined baking sheets and bake, rotating pans halfway through, until cookies are pale golden, about 20 minutes. Let cool.

**4** Meanwhile, make the glaze: Bring sugar, corn syrup, and 3 tbsp. water to a boil in a 1-qt. saucepan over high heat. Remove from the heat, add chocolate, and swirl pan to coat the chocolate with the sugar mixture. Let sit without stirring to allow the chocolate to melt, about 5 minutes. Slowly stir the chocolate with a rubber spatula until smooth; set aside to let cool slightly.

**5** Spoon about 1 tsp. of the filling onto 24 cookies, and top with remaining cookies. Gently press cookies together to sandwich them. Dip half of each cookie into the chocolate glaze. Transfer to a rack, and let the glaze solidify before serving.

## Strawberry Cake

SERVES 12

Vibrant cakes like this one, topped with strawberry cream cheese frosting, are part of the soul food tradition carried on by places like Martha Lou's Kitchen (page 15) and Bertha's

Kitchen, which provided this recipe, in Charleston, South Carolina.

16 tbsp. unsalted butter, softened, plus more for greasing pans
3 cups flour, plus more for pans
1 tbsp. baking powder
½ tsp. kosher salt
1 cup milk
½ cup seedless strawberry jam
3 tbsp. red food coloring (optional)
2 cups sugar
1 cup canola oil
1 tsp. vanilla extract
3 eggs
8 oz. cream cheese, softened
1 1-lb. box confectioners' sugar
1 tsp. strawberry extract

**1** Heat oven to 350°. Grease and flour two 9" round cake pans; set aside. Whisk together flour, baking powder, and salt in a medium bowl; set aside. Whisk together milk, jam, and 2 tbsp. food coloring in a small bowl; set aside. Beat together sugar, oil, vanilla, and eggs in a mixer on medium-high speed until pale and smooth, 2–3 minutes. In three additions, alternately add dry and wet ingredients to sugar mixture, beginning and ending with dry; mix until combined. Divide batter between prepared pans and smooth tops; bake until a toothpick inserted in the middle of cakes comes out clean, about 40 minutes. Let cool 15 minutes, unmold, then cool completely.

**2** In a large bowl, beat butter and cream cheese on high speed of a mixer until smooth and fluffy, 1–2 minutes. Add remaining food coloring, confectioners' sugar, and strawberry extract; beat until smooth.

**3** Place one cake upside down on a cake stand, and spread ⅓ frosting over top. Cover with second cake, top side up; frost top and sides of cakes with remaining frosting; refrigerate for 1 hour before serving. Let come to room temperature before serving.

## Sweet Porridge with Raisins and Almonds

*(Sheero)*

SERVES 6–8

This comforting dish enriched with clarified butter is cooked throughout the Indian state of Gujarat (page 108). Typically served as a dessert, it also makes a filling breakfast or snack.

1½ cups Indian durum wheat flour (also known as atta)
½ cup ghee or clarified butter, melted
1 tsp. ground cardamom
¼ cup sugar
¼ cup finely chopped jaggery or packed brown sugar
½ cup golden raisins
3 tbsp. chopped almonds

**1** Put flour into a 12" cast-iron skillet over medium heat and cook, stirring occasionally until toasted and sweetly fragrant, about 7 minutes.

**2** Add ghee, and stir vigorously until mixture is smooth and golden brown, about 1 minute. Stir in cardamom and 2 cups water; the mixture will thicken immediately. Reduce heat to medium-low; add sugar, jaggery, and raisins and cook, stirring occasionally, until the mixture has thickened and taken on the consistency of dry porridge, about 12 minutes. To serve, spoon porridge into bowls, and garnish with almonds.

# INDEX

# TABLE OF EQUIVALENTS

The exact equivalents in the following tables have been rounded for convenience.

**Liquid and Dry Measurements**

| U.S. | METRIC |
|---|---|
| ¼ teaspoon | 1.25 milliliters |
| ½ teaspoon | 2.5 milliliters |
| 1 teaspoon | 5 milliliters |
| 1 tablespoon (3 teaspoons) | 15 milliliters |
| 1 fluid ounce | 30 milliliters |
| ¼ cup | 65 milliliters |
| ⅓ cup | 80 milliliters |
| 1 cup | 235 milliliters |
| 1 pint (2 cups) | 480 milliliters |
| 1 quart (4 cups, 32 fluid ounces) | 950 milliliters |
| 1 gallon (4 quarts) | 3.8 liters |
| 1 ounce (by weight) | 28 grams |
| 1 pound | 454 grams |
| 2.2 pounds | 1 kilogram |

**Length Measures**

| U.S. | METRIC |
|---|---|
| ⅛ inch | 3 millimeters |
| ¼ inch | 6 millimeters |
| ½ inch | 12 millimeters |
| 1 inch | 2.5 centimeters |

**Oven Temperatures**

| FAHRENHEIT | CELSIUS | GAS |
|---|---|---|
| 250° | 120° | ½ |
| 275° | 140° | 1 |
| 300° | 150° | 2 |
| 325° | 160° | 3 |
| 350° | 180° | 4 |
| 375° | 190° | 5 |
| 400° | 200° | 6 |
| 425° | 220° | 7 |
| 450° | 230° | 8 |
| 475° | 240° | 9 |
| 500° | 260° | 10 |

# ACKNOWLEDGMENTS

I won't lie. Poring over the roughly 275,000 photographs that we edited down to those that appear in this book was a laborious process. It was also an absolute joy. Beside me virtually every step of the way was SAVEUR's art director, Dave Weaver. The realization of this project is as much due to him as anyone. I'd also like to thank deputy editors Betsy Andrews and Beth Kracklauer. It's Betsy's superb wordsmithery that gives the text in these pages its clarity and force; Beth's innate pursuit of excellence as an editor has ensured that word and image work together as powerfully as they possibly can. Executive food editor Todd Coleman curated the terrific roundup of recipes from SAVEUR's archives that comprise the last chapter, and, not insignificantly, also photographed a whole lot of the images that appear throughout. The efforts of managing editor Greg Ferro, an unparalleled pilot, to keep this book (and all of us) on track and on schedule cannot be underestimated. Among the other SAVEUR staff contributors are Karen Shimizu, associate editor, whose combined editing and fact-checking always keep us honest, and Chelsea Lobser, SAVEUR's photo director, whose brisk efficiency in delivering the images made it all possible; senior editor Gabriella Gershenson, test kitchen director Kellie Evans, associate food editor Ben Mims, assistant editor Marne Setton, pre-press director Don Hill, and copy editor Diane Hodges were likewise invaluable. Our friends at Weldon Owen—Hannah Rahill, Amy Marr, Emma Boys, Terry Newell, Kim Laidlaw, Kara Church, and Lauren Charles—proved once again to be great collaborators in putting together a book. Above all, I want to thank the photographers whose work appears herein (read more about them on page 268). They are not only the real heroes of this book, the work they do feeds this ever-expanding organism called SAVEUR every single day. —*James Oseland, editor-in-chief*

# THE PHOTOGRAPHERS

### ANDRE BARANOWSKI

Born and raised in Poland, Andre Baranowski has been taking photos since the seventh grade, when his father brought home a camera. Now based in New York, Baranowski has shot for *Departures* and many other magazines. More of his work can be seen at andrebaranowskiphoto.com.

### DAVID BRABYN

New York City–based David Brabyn studied politics and international relations in the UK and France before spending four years working as a freelance photojournalist in Africa, Southeast Asia, Central Europe, and the Middle East. See davidbrabyn.com for more of his work.

### TODD COLEMAN

SAVEUR executive food editor Todd Coleman travels all over the world to shoot for the magazine, and he props, styles, and shoots most of SAVEUR's covers. He has also photographed the cookbooks *The Japanese Grill* by Harris Salat and *The Mom 100* by Katie Workman.

### PENNY DE LOS SANTOS

Penny celebrates culture and community in her photography, and has received numerous awards for it. She has shot for *Time, National Geographic,* and many others. See more of her work at pennydelossantos.com, where you can also read her blogs about her assignments.

### NAOMI DUGUID

A contributing editor at SAVEUR, Naomi Duguid is the co-author of six award-winning books on food in its cultural context. Her latest work, *Burma: Rivers of Flavor,* celebrates the food cultures of Burma in recipes, stories and photos. She writes a weekly blog at naomiduguid.blogspot.com.

### ALI FARBOUD

As the son of an Iranian diplomat, Ali Farboud traveled extensively as a child and first started taking photos to document his travels. Today he is based in Los Angeles, London, and Tehran, where he shoots for a number of editorial and commercial clients.

### JAMES FISHER

Born and raised in rural Australia, James Fisher was introduced to photography by his grandfather. James's love of portraiture and indigenous cultures has taken him to many remote communities. He has shot for *Vanity Fair, GQ,* and others. More of his work can be seen at jamesfisher.com.au.

### ARIANA LINDQUIST

Ariana Lindquist is a documentary photographer whose honors include first-place awards from World Press Photo and a Fulbright to China. Her work appears in *Time, The New York Times,* and *The Atlantic,* among other publications. Visit arianalindquist.com to see more of her work.

**O. RUFUS LOVETT**

For the past 35 years O. Rufus Lovett has been living in Longview, Texas, where he teaches photography at Kilgore College. His work has appeared in *Texas Monthly, Gourmet,* and elsewhere. University of Texas Press has published two collections of his photography, *Weeping Mary* and *Kilgore Rangerettes.*

**REBECCA MCALPIN**

Rebecca started her career at a small-town newspaper in Michigan, covering county fairs and prom fashion shows. She now lives and works in New York City. Her work has appeared in *The New York Times, Food Arts,* and other publications. Visit rebeccamcalpin.com.

**LANDON NORDEMAN**

Landon Nordeman's award-winning photographs have appeared in *The New Yorker, National Geographic, Sports Illustrated,* and many other publications. He lives in New York City with his favorite subjects: his wife and son. Read more about Landon and his work at landonnordeman.com.

**JAMES OSELAND**

James has been the editor-in-chief of SAVEUR since 2006. Under his editorship, the magazine has won more than 30 awards, including two awards from the American Society of Magazine Editors. James is also a judge on Bravo TV's *Top Chef Masters.* More at jamesoseland.com.

**BARBARA RIES**

Barbara's images have won awards from the National Press Photographers and the White House News Photographers associations, and she has been named a Pulitzer Prize finalist in photography. Barbara lives in the San Francisco Bay Area. Visit barbararies.com to see more of her pictures.

**BETH ROONEY**

Chicago-based Beth Rooney is a freelance documentary photographer. Her images have appeared in *Time, The Chicago Tribune,* and *The New York Times,* among other places. More of her photographs can be viewed at bethrooney.com and beth rooneyphotography.com, where she keeps a blog.

**JUN TAKAGI**

Jun Takagi is based in the Tokyo area. He has worked for *Travel & Leisure, Food & Wine,* and SAVEUR, as well as various Japanese titles. He has also worked on the cookbooks *Svensk Smak Tokyo, Japanese Hot Pots,* and *The Japanese Grill.* More of his work can be seen at juntakagi.com.

**PALERMO, ITALY** Zia ("Aunt") Pina at her restaurant, which shares her name. *Photograph by Landon Nordeman*

270

Library of Congress Cataloging-in-Publication
data is available.

ISBN: 978-1-61628-440-4
Manufactured in China

10 9 8 7 6 5 4 3 2 1

Design by Dave Weaver

Conceived and published with SAVEUR by
Weldon Owen Inc.
415 Jackson Street, Suite 200, San Francisco, CA 94111
Telephone: 415 291 0100 Fax: 415 291 8841

www.weldonowen.com